T0219711

Designing Microservices with Django

An Overview of Tools and Practices

Akos Hochrein

Apress®

Designing Microservices with Django

Akos Hochrein
Berlin, Germany

ISBN-13 (pbk): 978-1-4842-5357-1   ISBN-13 (electronic): 978-1-4842-5358-8
https://doi.org/10.1007/978-1-4842-5358-8

Managing Director, Apress Media LLC: Welmoed Spahr
Acquisitions Editor: Celestin Suresh John
Development Editor: James Markham
Coordinating Editor: Aditee Mirashi

Cover designed by eStudioCalamar

Cover image designed by Freepik (www.freepik.com)

Distributed to the book trade worldwide by Springer Science+Business Media New York, 233 Spring Street, 6th Floor, New York, NY 10013. Phone 1-800-SPRINGER, fax (201) 348-4505, e-mail orders-ny@springer-sbm.com, or visit www.springeronline.com. Apress Media, LLC is a California LLC and the sole member (owner) is Springer Science + Business Media Finance Inc (SSBM Finance Inc). SSBM Finance Inc is a **Delaware** corporation.

For information on translations, please e-mail rights@apress.com, or visit http://www.apress.com/rights-permissions.

Apress titles may be purchased in bulk for academic, corporate, or promotional use. eBook versions and licenses are also available for most titles. For more information, reference our Print and eBook Bulk Sales web page at http://www.apress.com/bulk-sales.

Any source code or other supplementary material referenced by the author in this book is available to readers on GitHub via the book's product page, located at www.apress.com/978-1-4842-5357-1. For more detailed information, please visit http://www.apress.com/source-code.

Printed on acid-free paper

For my aunts

Table of Contents

About the Author

Akos Hochrein is a software engineer and technical lead. After receiving his degree in computer science, he started his career as a consultant and soon became a product developer at a well-known Hungarian startup, later moving to Berlin to dive into the local tech scene and to broaden his back-end architecture design experience. Throughout his career, he worked in areas such as front-end and back-end development, integrations, data streaming, and systems design. Occasionally, he shares his knowledge in various forums, such as technical conferences, his blog, . . . or a book.

About the Technical Reviewers

Balázs Tóthfalussy is a technical lead and software engineer, and former mentor of the author. After studying financial software development, he committed to the sector and expanded his knowledge as a Java developer. Later, he moved to China to extend his knowledge in agile development practices. There, he fell in love with Python, which he has been working with ever since. Today he leads a team of developers to deliver tooling to create a more pleasant experience for dozens of engineers at his company.

Csaba Okrona is a technology enthusiast, former software engineer, and current engineering manager. After leaving school, he started working for various Hungarian companies, eventually becoming the chief technical officer of one of the biggest Hungarian retail web sites. Pursuing his passion of people and tech, he moved into the startup scene and became an engineering manager, first of the author, then for the infrastructure team of a successful content management system in Berlin.

Acknowledgments

Writing down thoughts and creating a book is quite a difficult endeavor, and it requires a lot of people and luck to get it done. Luckily, I've had both on my side.

This is the place where I thank the entire Django community for being there and developing the basis of this book. Thank you! Stay awesome!

A thank you is in order to the publisher for helping me along the way and making sure I kept progressing even when I felt like no progress was being made. Thank you.

A big thank you is in order for the technical reviewers, Balázs and Csaba. They kept me focused and gave me great feedback on the direction and the contents of the book. They also aided me throughout my career to get to this point, for which I will always be grateful. Thank you! You are truly my friends.

I thank my friends here in Berlin and back in Budapest who kept me sane and pushed me through all the creative blocks I had throughout the writing process, even when I needed you to pay for the beer. Thank you. You know who you are.

Thanks need to go to my family as well, who encouraged me to follow my dreams and pushed me through difficult times in my life. Thanks Mom, Dad, and Zalán. I'm lucky to have you in my life.

Introduction

Welcome to *Designing Microservices with Django*. I decided to grab a pen and write this book because it was quite difficult for me to find easily digestible guides on how to design microservices, including some of the problems I might face along the way and the potential solutions to them.

I kick off this book by clarifying some of the terminology regarding service design. Together, we look at a couple of anecdotes that will help us understand the benefits and drawbacks of certain systems.

After that, we dive into Django development and develop an application for ourselves that we talk about later in the book. We examine various high-level concepts such as templates and view functions, in addition to lower level ones, such as permissions and user management.

Now armed with knowledge of Django development, we delve deeply into the different types of microservices and the high-level design principles we should follow when we design them. We also take a look at communication principles, such as REST (from the synchronous world) and AMQP (from the asynchronous world), to achieve an understanding of how these protocols work and which ones solve which sorts of problems.

Armed with microservice design knowledge, we study the methodologies and techniques of migrating code into smaller systems.

To close, we look at how we can scale our development by making tools that make microservices possible to all developers in a company. I hope you are excited about this journey. I certainly am; so let's get started!

CHAPTER 1

What are services?

Services have been around humanity since before the agricultural revolution. Whenever we go into a store or a restaurant, we are using a service. Some services are more complex than others and provide goods to us that are more tailored to our taste or require less effort to work with, whereas some of them are more specialized, focusing on a single task and doing that really well. Let's take a look at a simple example.

Both a market and a restaurant qualify as services, and even though, they provide us with different things, both of them give us the general item of food. When you enter a market, you can buy various ingredients from various sellers. Later on, you can combine all of these ingredients into various dishes of your liking at home. A fancy restaurant, however, will provide you with delicacies made on the spot. There are many processes and systems working in the backend of a restaurant, most of it you have no sense of, but after your request if processed, you get your meal delivered.

The restaurant/market-stall analogy is just one of many that we can bring up when we are talking about services. Conceptually, they work the same way as services in software.

1. You, the client, approach the service with a request.

2. The service, in our case the restaurant, receives your order.

© Akos Hochrein 2019
A. Hochrein, *Designing Microservices with Django*,
https://doi.org/10.1007/978-1-4842-5358-8_1

3. Some algorithms and processes in the background
    (the recipes and the chefs) prepare a response for
    you.

4. You receive the aforementioned response (most of
    the cases, at least).

A service could be your application that serves people on their phone
information on the number of times they left their home yesterday. Or a
service could be a massive continuous integration system that you only see
a small portion of that runs your application's tests. A service could also be
something tiny in software, an application that provides an interface to get
information about what time it is in Budapest, Hungary.

In this book, we are going to focus on services that reside on the web,
serving data to the end users and to other, internal services alike. Let's
begin by taking a look at the different definitions that emerged in the
industry.

Service Lingo

In the past couple of years, there has been a lot of buzz around service
design, software as a service, microservices, monoliths, service-oriented
architecture, and so on. In the next figure, it is plain to see that microservices
are becoming more and more popular. Figure 1-1 provides a graphical view
of Google searches of "microservices" over the past five years.

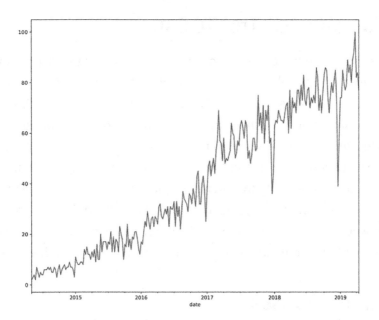

Figure 1-1. _Popularity of the term "microservices" since 2014, Google_

In the following sections we will try to make some sense on what each of these mean and what are the important terms you need to remember when you are working in systems like these. Please keep in mind that these terms are not etched into stone.

Software as a Service

The term "software as a service" (or SaaS) mostly describes a licensing model, where you can pay for the usage of some sort of online service. Most of these software live in the cloud and provide various ways for the end user to modify and query data in their systems. One example here is Spotify, an online music streaming software, which end users can use to listen to music and create their own playlist. Furthermore, Spotify has an extensive software interface and packages which engineers can use to fetch and modify data in the Spotify cloud programmatically.

Service-oriented Architecture

Service oriented architecture (or SoA) is probably one of the favourite terms in the industry. In simple terms, this style of architecture design supports services more than anything. A service, as we learned above, needs to serve some sort of business need and needs to be modeled around real world requirements. Services need to be self contained and have a clean interface with which they can be communicated with. They are deployed and developed independently and represent a unit of functionality on an abstract level. The architecture also involves the communication protocols used between these services. Some software as a service companies use service-oriented architecture to deliver quality products to their end users.

Monolithic Service

One of the dreaded words of the decade for software engineers. Monolithic applications and monolithic services are single services that grew too big to be able to reason about. What "too big" means exactly will be one of the core topics of this book. We will also see that this dreaded word does not necessarily mean something bad.

Microservice

The other dreaded word of the decade for software engineers (although, for different reasons). A microservice, in short, is a service that lives in a service-oriented architecture and is easy to reason about. These are loosely coupled, lightweight components which have a well defined interface, a single-purpose and are easy to create and dispose of. Due to the fine-grained nature, more people can work on them in parallel and ownership of features becomes a cleaner problem to solve for the organization.

Now that we've taken a look at the high level definitions, let's do a deep dive into monoliths.

Understanding the Monolith

As we've learned, monoliths are codebases that grew too big and too difficult to reason about by a single developer or even a team of developers, their complexity has reached a point where changing even just a couple of lines of code can have unintended and unknown consequences in other parts.

The first thing we need to lay down here as a foundation is that monoliths are not inherently bad. There are multiple companies that have built successful IT businesses on monolithic applications.

As a matter of fact, monoliths are actually great for growing your business. With small administrative overhead, you can add more features to your product. The ease of importing modules with just a couple of key combinations in your IDE makes development a breeze and gives you rushing confidence about delivering a lot of code (be it high quality or low quality) to your employer. Just like most growth processes in life, companies, and with that, software, needs to start fast and go through rapid iterations. Software needs quick growth so the business can get more money, so the software can grow more, so the business can get more money. You get where this is growing. So the next time you attend a conference and hear a speaker say that monoliths are systems of old design, make sure to take it with a pinch of salt. As a side note, I would like to mention, that if your startup is struggling with the maintenance of your legacy monolithic application, it is usually a sign of a healthy business.

However, tendency shows that this rapid growth tends to slow down as often over time reliability and scalability of software gets more and more important. Having a single application might earn your team fast deployment and easy-to-maintain infrastructure, but it also means that the mistake of a single engineer can bring down a whole application. The more people start working on a single application, the more they start disturbing each others work, the more they need to have unnecessary communication and the more they need to wait for their builds and deployments.

Imagine the following situation: you're an infrastructure engineer working for a company that streams videos as a service over the internet. The company is struggling, but somehow the CMO manages to get the government of your country to stream the presidential election speech. This is an amazing opportunity for your company to grow, so there's a lot of investment going into making sure that the system takes the load well. The weeks before the event, you've done plenty of load tests and instructed the backend engineers to fix certain parts of the code that is not performing as it is supposed to. You've convinced the COO to pour some money into heavier infrastructure, so the load will ease over the system. Everything looks perfect for the speech and you're anxiously waiting for it with your colleagues at the time of the event to experience the marvel of what you've been working on with such dedication in the past couple of weeks. Then it happens. Right before the speech, the stream stops. You have absolutely no idea what is happening and start furiously looking for answers. You try to SSH into the machines to no avail, getting rejected without remorse and the minutes are passing. It's been 13 minutes for the outage and the speech is nearly over. Twitter is on fire tagging your company on where they can watch the presidential speech and blaming the incompetence of the CEO. In a furious rage, decide to hard reset the machines on the cloud provider website that you're using, but it's too little too late. The event is over. Millions are disappointed and the company is not in a very good shape to get the next round of investment. 2 days later you get back to work and start doing some investigation on what had happened. Turns out, the ads team has rolled out some changes 2 days earlier that caused a memory leak in the backend application. The memory on the servers got full and blocked all processes. This was when you started dreaming of a better and more reliable future for your company's infrastructure.

Figure 1-2 is a simple illustration of what had happened at this video streaming company in the application.

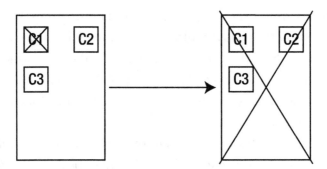

Figure 1-2. *A full outage caused by a tightly coupled broken component*

The story above, albeit completely made up, happens in the life cycle of every successful software system and every successful software company. If you think Facebook or Google have never had hour long outages at important moments in their lifetime, you're very much wrong. You can find documentation about various Google[1] outages online, with (sometimes) detailed descriptions on what parts of the system caused this and that parts to be down for this and that amount of time. After these outages they learn, adapt and make their systems more resilient so the same problem doesn't occur again.

There is an aspect of monolithic applications that many people don't think about that I like to call the "monolithic waterfall" or "cascading monolith" architectures. This basically means that when you're working on a monolithic application you're almost encouraged to design the architecture of your code and your data in a monolithic way. Designing interfaces around your modules becomes a chore and just overhead, so you just import the line that you need. Adding a new database for subscription information takes way too much time and would just introduce more complexity, so you create the models in the

---

[1]https://googleblog.blogspot.com/2014/01/todays-outage-for-several-google.html

same database as your user and product information resides. If you're working on a monolith, all layers of your code and architecture will be monolithic. Naturally, strict coding guidelines, architecture principles and a challenging engineering culture can build and maintain a monolith with clear internal interface boundaries that can later be broken down into microservices with more ease.

Now, it would not be fair to not mention the benefits of monoliths again here at the end of this part. All horror stories above and negativities aside, the recommendation is to grow your business and your engineering by utilizing the monolithic model. Just make sure to keep a tight grip on the steering wheel and everyone is on the same page about technical debt.

Now that we have an understanding of how a monolith looks and acts like, we will take a look at it's counterpart for the book, the microservice.

Understanding the Microservice

Just to recap: a microservice is a single purpose software application that resides somewhere on the web, is a small-ish codebase and can be reasoned about easily even by a single engineer.

Just like we learned about monoliths that they are not the spawn of Satan, we are going to learn about microservices that they are not a silver bullet either.

Let's go back to our infrastructure engineer in the previous story. After the incident he ran a post mortem (if you don't exactly know what that is, don't worry, we will explore it later in the book) with the rest of the company and came to the conclusion that one of the best solutions that the company could take to avoid such catastrophes as they had a couple of weeks ago during the New Year's Speech, is to adapt and implement a microservice based architecture and leave the monolith behind. He outlined the costs that it would take from the engineers and the investors and made sure that everyone understands the benefits and drawbacks of a migration. Soon later, the board gave a go to the project. Some time later the company already had a dozen of services running in the cloud (still including the remainders of the monolith), and another campaign kicked in. This time the load was high, but the system kept resilient. Despite the chat services going down, the video playback still worked, making sure that the company reputation is intact and the investors have put their money in a good place. Our engineer went back to bed knowing that there will be no issues ever again around the core business and lived happily ever after. In the following figure 1-3, we can see how we lost our coupled architecture from our previous figure and only have a partial outage now.

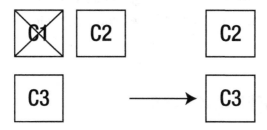

Figure 1-3. *Components that are loosely coupled might only cause partial outages*

Is that it? Well, no. In the above story our company had a service that ran the chat systems, but the core business was still most likely residing in the monolith. If the chat system were there, it is completely possible that this marketing campaign would have been a disaster as well, causing the end of the company for real. In conclusion, building or extracting even small modules in your system can cause big wins in critical situations.

You can hear dozens of these amazing stories when you go to conferences, I myself gave a couple of them. In most of these success stories there is a small but significant thing that the presenters (including myself) don't really like to talk about. This is the amount of time that was invested into making sure that a systems that is described above works on a software level and works on an organizational level as well. In most cases implementing a working microservice architecture takes years of engineering work which involves not just coding, but architectural plans, vast amounts of tooling, research of current systems, release plans, meetings, meetings and meetings, and last but not least, patience.

Keep in mind that a switch like this can be an excellent way to enable engineers in your organization to grow and to test their knowledge not just in technical but organizational matters as well. It's a great opportunity to retain senior engineers at your company and to enable regulars and juniors to explore new frontiers of the full stack that they didn't need to touch yet.

At this point, it might seem like a great idea to start your entre architecture with microservices. Let's explore this option in the next section.

Early Design Choices

Speaking from experience, one of the biggest mistakes a company can make nowadays is starting building their architecture using microservices. Albeit the tooling of today is vastly superior to the tooling of let's say 5 years ago. We have amazing orchestrators, like Kubernetes, containerization tools, like Docker, various services on AWS, like EBS that help us build and deploy services. However, despite the amazing tooling, development could go to hell very quickly.

The thing that a business needs in the beginning (as we already talked about this briefly) is agility. Rapid changes on the data, logic and presentation level to ship as many user features as possible. Designing and building services, on the other hand, take time, dedication and hardcore processes. Subsequently, starting your engineering culture and development processes with a microservice architecture might lead to a disaster.

I myself worked in a system that was designed from the get go to be "microservice" oriented. On paper, everything looked fantastic. The services had clear interface definitions and all of them had owners. These services got compiled together and communicated with each other through an asynchronous, event based system. The build process used a very established build orchestrator as the base system and was optimized to help all the engineers succeed. After so much praise you can expect that the result was negative. Yes, it was. Everything looked perfect in theory, but most of the things failed in practice. The systems were too distributed and dependencies became a burden instead of enablers. Engineers needed speed and not a system where they needed to bump versions every single component when they updated another one. Maintaining the interface definitions became a nightmare after a while as it was difficult to understand cross-dependencies and versioning among the components. Engineers were looking for customized and unregulated shortcuts more than they were engaged in the current working methods. The build system, albeit very professional, was deemed to be too early for it's time, slowing down developers more than enabling them to speed up development.

Later on the company decided to merge together the microservice architecture into a monolithic application and things started to speed up afterwards. Ultimately proving the system to be successful. Eventually the codebase grew too big and teams started to think about ways of splitting it again.

Was it a bad idea to start with microservices? Was it a good idea to move to a monolith, whereas the engineering norms dictate that you should be moving into another direction?

The answer to the first question is not so obvious. If the company was bigger, the engineering culture was designed around this type of architecture, and there would've been more time invested into tooling, then probably it would've worked out. However, mid to small size companies often cannot afford the dedicated engineers for tooling.

Large companies, with spare capacity on their hand, on the other hand can design their systems using these philosophies from the get-go.

As for the second question, no matter who you ask, the answer will be a resounding yes. In this story, one of the great exemplars is the ability to be able to look back and take two steps backwards to make a gigantic leap forwards on the long run.

One of the morals of the story is that in order to make this leap, you need to understand not only the technologies and the best practices in the industry, but you also need to understand your business, organization and the people who work at your company as well. What might work for other companies (and in some cases even just other teams in your engineering organization) might be a huge misstep for you.

Summary

In this chapter, we have learned the basic linguistics that you can use when talking to your colleagues about microservices over office coffee. We've also learned that monoliths are not inherently bad, they can even help grow your business just as rapidly as microservices can slow you down if you use them at the wrong time, but in the long run, can change the way how your users interact with your systems for the better. In the rest of the book, we are going to explore exactly what is required of you, the engineer, product owner, architect, to make sure that adapting to this mindset of development will be a good addition to your company and not an agile disaster.

CHAPTER 2

A Pinch of Django

One of the most important considerations that one needs to make when designing software services is the programming language and the frameworks associated with it to use during the project.

For educational purposes in this book we are going to use the Python programming language with the Django Web Framework and associated toolchains to achieve our goals. To catch up out knowledge a little bit, we are going to go through the core concepts of Django and build a service ourselves.

Introducing the Problem

In this book, we will aim to stay to problems that are as close to real life as possible. So we are going to work with business requirements and try to follow the service design progression of an entire product, not just tiny parts of it. Here is our problem space for the following pages:

Tizza. Tizza is a mobile first application in which users can decide by photographs and descriptions of pizzas if they like them or not. Upon liking a place, the user will receive notifications of group visits organized to the given pizza place using the application. The end user has a friends list, which they should be able to manage. There can be settings for private (friends only) and public (not just friends) events by the user.

© Akos Hochrein 2019
A. Hochrein, *Designing Microservices with Django*,
https://doi.org/10.1007/978-1-4842-5358-8_2

Naturally, our company needs to make money somehow. For this, we collect advertisement/ranking money from pizza places to be on our platform. Depending on a sales system, we need to determine where a company stands in our rankings and what order the end users should see the restaurants.

Getting Started

Right before we get heavily into service design, we are going to run a couple of commands in our terminal to get started with our Django project.

Note   it is highly recommended to structure your code and dependencies into virtual environments or containers. If you are not entirely familiar with these concepts, I highly recommend checking out Python development with virtualenv or Docker.

To install Django, all you need to do is run the following code in your terminal:

```
pip install django
```

When we see a Django application running as a whole, we call that a project. To create a Django project, you simply need to execute the following command in your terminal:

```
django-admin startproject tizza
```

With this, a simple Django application will be created in a folder called tizza, as shown in Figure 2-1.

tizza
  - manage.py
  - tizza
      - settings.py
      - urls.py
      - wsgi.py

Figure 2-1. *Bare django folder structure*

What if I told you that at this point you already have a functioning website? Type the following in your terminal:

```
python manage.py runserver
```

And in your browser access *http://localhost:8000*

You should see the screen in Figure 2-2.

Figure 2-2. *Django has successfully been installed*

Congratulations! Now the real work starts.

Django Apps

Django has a second layer of logic in its general folder structure. These are called apps. The naming might be a bit confusing, since they have nothing to do with software running on your smartphones. Apps are usually used as logical separators between business cases and/or features in your application. You can think of projects as being able to orchestrate between different apps, whereas one app can only belong to one project. To create a new app, we simply need to run the following command:

```
python manage.py startapp pizza
```

Now our directory structure has been updated as shown in Figure 2-3.

tizza
- manage.py
- tizza
  ...
- pizza
  - admin.py
  - apps.py
  - migrations
    ...
  - models.py
  - tests.py
  - views.py

Figure 2-3. *Bare django folder structure with app*

Some applications are by default in Django projects, so we don't need to deal with them every single time we create a new project. They are installed with Django itself, that's why you don't see them in the folder structure. One of these is the auth application that contains tools for user creation and authorization. Another one that we are going to utilize heavily is the admin package, which gives us a great deal of control over the data of our application.

Models and the Power of ORMs

Whenever you receive a new feature or start working on an entirely new product or application, the first thing you usually need to think about is the data that is going to drive it. Once the data is figured out, with the power of Django and ORMs, we can get started immediately.

What are ORMs?

ORMs (or Object Relational Mappings) serve as an abstraction layer between the database and your application. You don't want to create marshaling and unmarshaling code every time you run a raw query on a database. We are not only talking about issues of bugs, but also huge security problems that these unprotected systems can have.

Instead, we are going to use ORMs, most languages and web frameworks have something similar in place. For Python developers that don't use Django (or don't need an entire web framework), there's SQLAlchemy. For PHP developers there's Doctrine, for Ruby enthusiasts ActiveRecord. In short, I strongly recommend to start using and get used to ORMs, if you haven't already, as they will make your and other developers life in your company much simpler.

To give you a bit more on ORMs, imagine the following situation: you're an engineer fresh out of school, eager to work the living hell out of your first job, which is the maintenance and extension of a web application. The first task that you get is to fetch and display some data from the database. Luckily you took database and networking classes, so you have a vague idea on how the data should be flowing. The first piece of code you write is shown in Listing 2-1.

Listing 2-1. Simple query to get a pizza

```
import database

def get_pizzas(pid):
    cursor = database.cursor()
    return cursor.execute(f"""
SELECT * FROM pizzas WHERE id = {pid};
""")
```

The code is not awful, per se, however, there are a couple of pretty serious issues with it that experienced engineers might have noticed already:

1. Security. If the pizza id comes from the user (and most likely it comes), they can simply drop the entire database with a clever injection here. If you want extra security with raw queries, you need to implement it yourself. Could be a good exercise for you, however, it's definitely an awful one for your business.

2. Maintainability: Working with text objects is ... well, difficult to say the least. In the above piece of code you are hiding a condition in a text and no IDE will be able to help you with refactoring it. Also, if the query grows, the headache grows with it. Another aspect you might want to consider here is maintenance of multiple database engines. If you would like to change your database from Postgres to MySQL, you might need to update all the queries manually, which can be very error-prone.

All in all, writing code like the above one is dangerous and brings unnecessary risks for both data integrity and engineering longevity.

Naturally, some problems cannot be solved with the methods we are going to be looking at, in those cases you can always fall back to raw SQL queries, just be extra mindful of what you're typing.

The Pizza

In Django, we need to create a models.py file in our application to get started with our ORMs. The file should look something like this:

Listing 2-2. Database model for our pizza

```
# pizza/models.py
from django.db import models

class Pizza(models.Model):
    title = models.CharField(max_length=120)
    description = models.CharField(max_length=240)
```

What you can see above is a manifestation of a database table as a Django model. The Pizza class inherits from the Model class provided by Django. This will notify the system that there is a new data type that we would like to use, with the fields that we list in the next couple of lines. In our case a title and a description that are both character fields. Keeping it simple for now, we are going to create our table in the database. For which we are going to use the power of migrations.

Migrations

Migrations are nothing less than generated scripts from your models that you can use to automagically scaffold your databases, without running manual **CREATE TABLE** and such operations. Migrations are an incredibly powerful tool that I recommend reading more about, for the purpose of this book, we are only going to use the basics.

```
python manage.py makemigtations
```

19

Running the above command in your project directory will cause Django to collect the models in each application that is registered in the settings file under **insalled_apps** and then create a migration plan for them. Migration plans are essentially Python files that contain database operations in order of execution that will run on the database. That is, if you run the following command:

```
python manage.py migrate
```

Now your tables should be in place, it's time for us to explore what we have in our database.

A Bit More on Migrations...

So you just created a model, ran 2 commands in your shell and suddenly you have a database setup with all the tables you'd like to work with. What just happened? How is life so amazing?

What Django does is *actually* pretty incredible. When you run the makemigrations command, Django collects all the models that were created in your applications (per application), registers them in memory and parses their metadata, such as the columns, indexes and sequences that are required in it. After that it runs a code generation module that will create a diff between the previous state of you database meta information and the current one and renders a file for in the migrations folder. This file is a simple Python file that should probably look something like this:

Listing 2-3. Migration file for the initial pizza

```
from django.db import migrations, models

class Migration(migrations.Migration):
    initial = True
    dependencies = [
    ]
```

```
operations = [
    migrations.CreateModel(
        name='Pizza',
        fields=[
            ('id', models.AutoField(auto_created=True,
            primary_key=True, serialize=False, verbose_
            name='ID')),
            ('title', models.CharField(max_length=120)),
            ('description', models.CharField(max_
            length=240)),
        ],
    ),
]
```

You can view it and modify it to your needs. Make sure to take a look at the migration file that was created in the migrations folder in the pizza app. Try adding a new field to the model, run makemigrations again and see the differences between the 2 files that were created.

When you apply the migrations with the migrate command, you just basically execute these Python files in order using a database engine. One thing to note here, is that running migrations might be an expensive operation on your live database, depending on the size of the tables, the allocated resources and the complexity of the migration of course. I always recommend to be mindful when executing migrations in a live environment!

Migrations were not always part of core Django. For a long amount of time we had to use external tools or just raw SQL scripts to generate the databases. Nowadays almost all major frameworks have one way or another to run migrations. Make sure to explore the documentation for further technicalities!

Simple ORM Examples

Accessing the way your project is going to behave when it's running is quite simple. just execute:

```
python manage.py shell
```

This will start up an interactive Python REPL which has all the settings loaded from your Django application and behaves exactly as your application would in the current context.

```
>>> from pizza.models import Pizza
>>> Pizza.objects.all()
<QuerySet []>
```

We can see that there are no pizzas currently in the database, so let's create one:

```
>>> Pizza.objects.create(title="Pepperoni and Cheese",
description="Best pizza ever, clearly")
<Pizza: Pizza object (1)>
>>> Pizza.objects.all()|
<QuerySet [<Pizza: Pizza object (1)>]>
>>> pizza = Pizza.objects.get(id=1)
>>> pizza.title
'Pepperoni and Cheese'
```

Creating a new object in our data storage is this easy. Updating an existing one is just as simple.

```
>>> pizza.description
'Best pizza ever, clearly'
>>> pizza.description = "Actually the best pizza ever."
>>> pizza.save()
```

```
>>> pizza2 = Pizza.objects.get(id=1)
>>> pizza2.description
'Actually the best pizza ever.'
```

Now with this example we are quite lucky, however, we didn't really meet any business needs yet, so let's keep on adding a couple of models to at least satisfy some of the requirements amidst the immense fun we are having:

Listing 2-4. Extended models file for our application

```
# pizza/models.py
from django.db import models

from user.models import UserProfile

class Pizzeria(models.Model):
    owner = models.ForeignKey(UserProfile, on_delete=models.
    CASCADE)
    address = models.CharField(max_length=512)
    phone = models.CharField(max_length=40)

class Pizza(models.Model):
    title = models.CharField(max_length=120)
    description = models.CharField(max_length=240)
    thumbnail_url = models.URLField()
    approved = models.BooleanField(default=False)
    creator = models.ForeignKey(Pizzeria, on_delete=models.
    CASCADE)

class Likes(models.Model):
    user = models.ForeignKey(UserProfile, on_delete=models.
    CASCADE)
    pizza = models.ForeignKey(Pizza, on_delete=models.CASCADE)
```

In the meantime, we have created a new app called auth in which we've added a model called the UserProfile. In Django, it is quite common to extend the already existing and perfectly functioning User model this way. Newer versions of Django also offer different methods of extending the already existing user model, you can read more about these on the official Django website (https://www.djangoproject.com/). Since we are already experienced Django programmers, we know that using the UserProfile as a foreign key is usually a more stable practice than using the User model, due to its flexibility. Make sure that after every model change, you run the makemigrations and the migrate commands to keep your database up-to-date.

Now that we've created a good number of models, we can play around a little bit more with the shell in Exercise 2-1.

EXERCISE 2-1: PLAY WITH THE SHELL

Create a couple of new pizzas in the shell and put them under a newly created pizzeria. Try to get all the pizzas of a pizzeria. Create a couple of likes for a pizza. Try to access all the likes of a pizzeria! These are all great features that could one day be part of our application. Feel free to explore the shell and the model layer.

Communication with Views

The primary way of exposing our data is going to be with the use of Django's views. Views are essentially endpoints that you can utilize to return various types of data to your customers, including the HTML pages in their browsers.

To set up a view, we are going to create a file called **views.py** in the **pizza** app.

Listing 2-5. The first view we've created to return pizzas

```python
# pizza/views.py
from django.http import HttpResponse

from .models import Pizza

def index(request, pid):
    pizza = Pizza.objects.get(id=pid)
    return HttpResponse(
        content={
            'id': pizza.id,
            'title': pizza.title,
            'description': pizza.description,
        }
    )
```

We will also need to add an url for this. We can do this by creating and editing a **urls.py** file in the **pizza** and the **tizza** module.

Listing 2-6. The edited urls files so we can access the resources

```python
# pizza/urls.py
from django.urls import include, path

from .views import index

urlpatterns = [
    path('<int:pid>', index, name='pizza'),
]

# tizza/urls.py
from django.contrib import admin
from django.urls import include, path
```

```
urlpatterns = [
    path('admin/', admin.site.urls),
    path('pizzas/', include('pizza.urls')),
]
```

Excellent! It's high time that we start accessing the data using the power of the internet. Depending on what type of tools you're using, you can make a remote call to the pizzas endpoint. Here's a curl you can run from your terminal:

```
curl http://localhost:8000/pizzas/1
```

You can also just enter it in your browser, it's still going to work.

Note   curl is a command line tool to do various operations with URLs, we are going to use it throughout the book to test our endpoints and code. It is recommended to get somewhat familiar with it. Check it out at `https://ec.haxx.se/`.

If you can see the id, description and the title of the pizza that we've created just a few minutes ago, I've great news for you: you've successfully queried the database through the internet! If you had problems, I recommend checking if your server is running and if not, running the following command before trying again:

```
python manage.py runserver
```

Now, let's try out the following:

```
curl http://localhost:8000/pizzas/42
```

Yeah, this doesn't really work. If we want to return a proper response, we need to modify the view function (Exercise 2-2).

EXERCISE 2-2: FIX THE UGLY 42

The view function for pizzas is actually pretty bad now. It took us roughly 15 seconds to find a pretty nasty bug. Luckily we have the weekend to work on this, so let's make sure that if one of our clients call the endpoint for a non-existent pizza, we return a reasonable response, such as:

```
{
    "status": "error",
    "message": "pizza not found"
}
```

Our view function looks great, but we will need some extra functionality to adhere to the business requirements (Exercise 2-3).

EXERCISE 2-3: RANDOM PIZZAS

Let's create an endpoint that will return a random pizza from the database. The endpoint should have the following path:

```
/pizzas/random
```

Let's make sure that we don't mess up the other endpoints while doing this!

After we are done, we can also return 15 random pizzas to the client (so we won't make that many remote calls to the backend server). We should also make sure that if a user has seen a pizza, they should not receive the same one again. You can probably use the **Likes** model for this.

The Admin Panel

You might have noticed, that we've added a url called **admin** to our url patterns. Django comes with a very handy admin view to the entire application by default. This can be quite useful if you need to manage objects in the database by hand. To access the admin panel, first you will need to create a superuser in the database.

```
python manage.py createsuperuser
```

Add the credentials that you'd like to log in with, start the development server (if not already running), and log in as the admin user on the /**admin** url. A superuser will have access to everything on the admin site, it's your first entry point to the system.

At this point you will probably not see a lot of useful modules apart from the user management. If you'd like to work with pizza resources here, you need to add the following code to **tizza/pizza/admin.py**, that will tell the admin panel to register the pizza model for administration.

```
from django.contrib import admin

from .models import Pizza

class PizzaAdmin(admin.ModelAdmin):
    pass

admin.site.register(Pizza, PizzaAdmin)
```

At this point we can access the Django admin panel and see how our models are behaving on a UI (Figure 2-4).

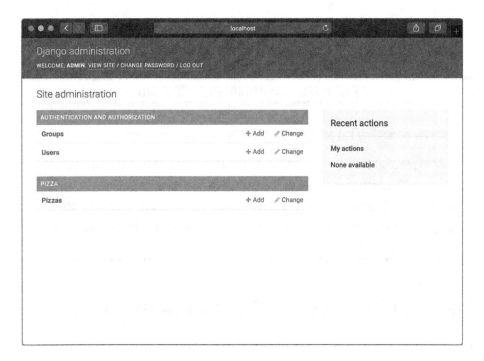

Figure 2-4. *The Django admin panel*

On this screen, you can access all user information, all models that are registered in Django, including user groups and permissions as well. Overall quite handy and a very powerful tool for aiding customers quickly.

It's also an excellent tool for testing purposes when you're checking if your application is working correctly or not. Creating a user becomes a non-technical task just a couple of clicks away.

The admin panel is also a highly configurable interface. You can add custom fields and custom actions to various models that you've implemented. If you'd like to learn more about the Django admin, I recommend checking the documentation. There's still a lot to explore here.

Note   If you want access to the live database this way, you will need to create a superuser for each environment.

To make sure that we get comfortable with the admin panel, let's create a couple of users and a couple of pizzas in Exercise 2-4.

EXERCISE 2-4: ADMIN PLAYGROUND

Let's try accessing the pizzas from the APIs that we've created.

Just to practice the versatility of the admin application, let's add a new field to pizzas, with which we can select if the pizza is with meat, vegetarian or vegan. Hint: for the database model, you should check out models.ChoiceField. After adding it, run the migrations and try creating a new pizza in the admin panel. What has changed?

Logging in, Logging Out and Signing up

Before we go any further, we really need to enable our users to sign up, log in and log out of our systems. Let's put together a quick app for that, shall we?

Signing up

Probably we would like to give some means to our users to sign up before we want them to log in (not always the case, but in this one, we shall do this).

Django provides quite a powerful toolset to implement a simple registration form for your users.

First off, we are going to create a view for signing up. But where should we put it? I guess user app should be fine for now. We will be using Django forms to solve this issue, as the auth app provides a form for signing up users by default.

```
from django.contrib.auth.forms import UserCreationForm
```

For assigning the user a session and making sure that they are who they claim to be, we are going to use the **login** and **authenticate** helpers from the **auth** app.

```
from django.contrib.auth import login, authenticate
```

At this point, it's a matter of gluing these functions together. To make our system a bit more flexible, we are going to use class based views, also provided by Django:

Listing 2-7. Class based view for signing up

```
# user/views.py
from django.contrib.auth import login, authenticate
from django.contrib.auth.forms import UserCreationForm
from django.shortcuts import render, redirect
from django.views import View

class SignupView(View):
    template_name = 'signup.html'

    def post(self, request):
        if form.is_valid():
            form.save()
            username = form.cleaned_data.get('username')
            password = form.cleaned_data.get('password1')
            user = authenticate(username=username,
            password=password)
            login(request, user)
            return redirect('/')

    def get(self, request):
        return render(request, self.template_name, {'form':
        UserCreationForm()})
```

As you can see, class based views are a more concise way of describing what can happen on your endpoint depending on the action you are using on it. We just need a screen now where we display this to the users.

Listing 2-8. Template for the sign up form

```
{# user/templates/signup.html #}

{% block content %}
<h2>Sign up</h2>
<form method="post">
{% csrf_token %}
    {{ form.as_p }}
    <button type="submit">Sign up</button>
</form>
{% endblock %}
```

This is a template document that is written using the jinja2 template language. You can see that most of it looks like regular HTML. There are replaceable blocks defined with the {% block ... %} operators and we are injecting values from the backend at render-time with the {{ ... }} tags. We also use a special tag for the csrf token, which is used to make sure that only authorized entities can use our form, it's required by Django. The as_p method will render your form as elements that are listed as paragraphs. Now, all we need to do is to make sure that we have the endpoint exposed.

```
from django.urls import path
from tizza.user.views import SignupView

urlpatterns = [
    path(r'^register/$', SignupView.as_view()),|
]
```

Excellent. Using the as_view method, we can easily convert our class based view to a regular Django view that we encountered earlier in the chapter. You can see the sign up page that we've created in Figure 2-5.

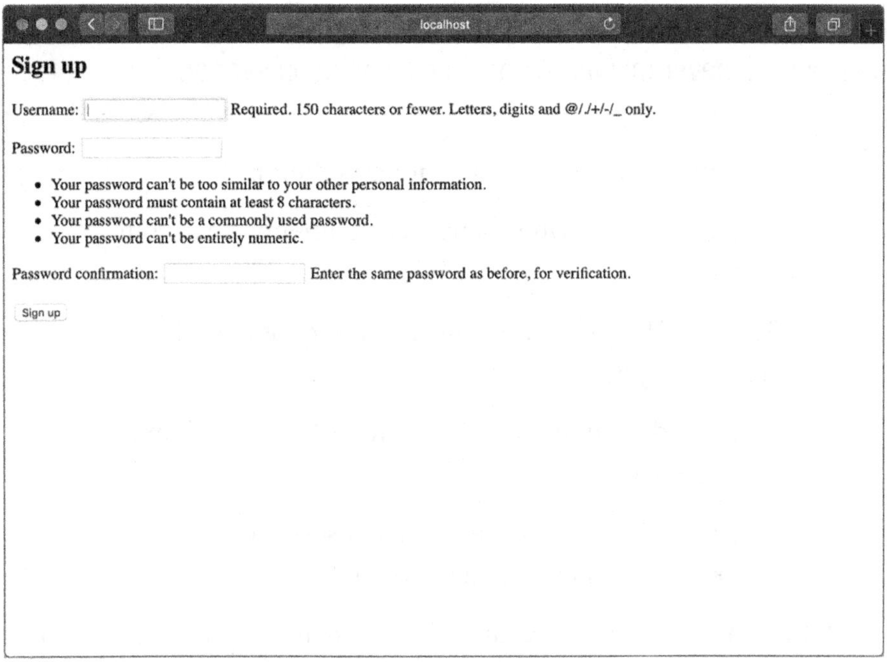

Figure 2-5. *The sign up page*

Login and Logout

As we've seen before, the **auth** package provided by Django comes with a lot of built in functionalities. These include the client side authentication endpoints as well.

Note   Authentication vs authorization: It's quite common to confuse authentication and authorization. The easiest way of discerning the two is the following: **authentication** verifies **who** you are, whereas **authorization** says **what** you can do in a system. Just remember this and you will never mix them up in a conversation ever again.

The following ones are included (amongst others):

- **/login** - The page where a user can authenticate to your systems.

- **/logout** - The page where the user can de-authenticate from your system.

- **/password_change** - The page where users can change their password.

- **/password_reset** - The page where users can reset their password if they have forgotten it.

Adding these endpoints to your system is not the hardest thing to do, all we need to change is the **urls.py** file in the project directory.

Listing 2-9. Urls for logging in and logging out

```
# tizza/urls.py
from django.contrib import admin
from django.urls import include, path
from django.contrib.auth import views as auth_views

urlpatterns = [
    path('admin/', admin.site.urls),
    path('pizzas/', include('pizza.urls')),
```

```
    path('login/', auth_views.login, name='login'),
    path('logout/', auth_views.logout, name='logout'),
]
```

By default, Django will attempt to render the **registration/login. html** template. Let's create this file in the following format., which is quite similar to the sign up page:

```
{% block title %}Login{% endblock %}

{% block content %}
  <h2>Login</h2>
  <form method="post">
    {% csrf_token %}
    {{ form.as_p }}
    <button type="submit">Login</button>
  </form>
{% endblock %}
```

Now that we've added the authentication urls to the urlpatterns, we will need to create a couple of pages to make sure that users can log in to our systems.

Let's extend now the **pizzas** endpoints a little bit more, since we will need to be able to interact with them.

First, we are going to add a pizza creation endpoint for users who own pizzerias, this could be done in a myriad of ways, this time we are going to use HTTP verbs to differentiate between the various actions that we would like to do on our entities.

Listing 2-10. Extended pizzas endpoint

```python
# pizza/views.py
import json

from django.contrib.auth.decorators import login_required
from django.http import HttpResponse

from .models import Pizza

@login_required
def index(request, pid):
    if request.method == 'POST':
        data = json.loads(request.body)
        new_pizza = Pizza.objects.create(
            title=data['title'], description=data
            ['description'],
            creator=request.user,
        )
        new_pizza.save()
        return HttpResponse(
            content={
                'id': new_pizza.id,
                'title': new_pizza.title,
                'description': new_pizza.description,
            }
        )
    elif request.method == 'GET':
        pizza = Pizza.objects.get(id=pid)
        return HttpResponse(
            content={
                'id': pizza.id,
                'title': pizza.title,
```

```
            'description': pizza.description,
        }
    )
```

There, now with our logged in user we can create a new Pizza. The code is a bit on a mess, but we can fix it later, right? Riiiight. What you can also see up there is that I've used a decorator to ensure that only logged in users can create pizzas. There are various decorators and class based view mixins provided by Django by default. I recommend checking them out and choosing ones that are appropriate to your usage. Decorators are very-very powerful tools when designing services, we will definitely encounter them later in the book.

You can also notice a subtle thing that I was able to do with the power of the **login_required** decorator. This is nothing less than using the **request.user**, which was populated by the **AuthenticationMiddleware**. Wait, what is a middleware?

A Primer on Middlewares

Middlewares are one of the core concepts of Django. Just like ogres and onions, Django also has layers that your request and response goes through when they enter and exit your application. The centerpiece of this layered system is the view function and the class based view itself. Consider Figure 2-6.

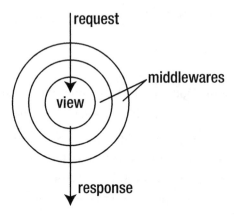

Figure 2-6. *Django request response cycle at a glance*

Here you can see that when a request comes into your application, it enters the various middleware layers that can do plenty of things with them. A couple of examples for middlewares:

AuthenticationMiddleware - Ensures that the **request.user** object exists and you can access it. If the user is logged in then it will be populated with the user object. If not, then an anonymous user will be sitting on this attribute. Oftentimes it is sery convenient to subclass this middleware and extend it with other user related data, such as from the **UserProfile** which we mentioned earlier.

SecurityMiddleware - Provides various security related features, such as HTTPS redirects, redirect blocking, xss protection.

CommonMiddleware - Provides some basic functionalities that are chores to implement. Such as sending away banned user-agents and making sure that the URL ends with a slash.

As you can see, middlewares have a wide variety of uses, be cautious with what you put in the codebase of a middleware, though. Since all requests in your service will enter that middleware, computation intensive and network operations might slow down your application significantly.

EXERCISE 2-5: RATE LIMITING MIDDLEWARE

If you're following along with tizza, you know that our fictional enterprise is growing rapidly at this point. With high growth, comes high traffic and our servers can barely hold the load. New machines will be provided in a couple of weeks, however, we need a solution until that time. Create a middleware that limits the number of calls from the same IP address over a certain period of time to a configurable number in the Django settings. As a bonus, check if you can use the decorator pattern to be more mindful of which endpoints you would like to protect.

EXERCISE 2-6: LIKING PIZZAS

Remember when we were extending our pizzas endpoint with returning an array of random pizzas depending if the user has seen them or not? Well, good news, now we actually have the tools to implement the "liking" functionality. So, your task is going to be to create an endpoint that can either "like" or "dislike" a certain pizza by the logged in user. It might be necessary to edit our models as well to make this work. Luckily we are early in the project.

Templates

Now that we're familiar with how Django works deep down and we've created a couple of simple pages that can be accessed through a browser, let's dive a bit deeper in how we can make the user-experience a bit more bearable, before our company can afford a designer.

As we've seen in the login form, the main channel of communication between the Django backend and our users happen through templates (and, well Javascript, but we will get back to that later). Let's remind ourselves quickly what a template actually looks like:

Listing 2-11. Reminder on templates

```
{# user/templates/signup.html #}
{% extends 'base.html' %}

{% block content %}
<h2>Sign up</h2>
<form method="post">
{% csrf_token %}
    {{ form.as_p }}
    <button type="submit">Sign up</button>
</form>
{% endblock %}
```

The first line is a comment, if you're reading this book, you're probably already familiar with comments.

The second line is an extends statement. It basically means that this template is going to use all the blocks from the template that is registered as base.html and then extend and override the attributes that are specified in that. What this means, is that we can build a base template for our application, where we need to specify parts of the website that need to happen everywhere only once. Let's look at a quick example:

Listing 2-12. Simple base template

```
<html>
    <head>
        <meta charset="utf-8"/>
        {% block css %}{% endblock %}
    </head>
```

```
{% block header %}
<header>This is the header of the website, the designers
will probably want it to be sticky and we need to add a
login button to the right if the customer is logged our or
a logout button if they are logged in</header>
{% endblock %}

{% block content %}
{% endblock %}

{% block footer %}
<footer>This will be our footer where we will put columns
about our company values and the job openings.</footer>
{% endblock %}

{% block javascript %}{% endblock %}
</html>
```

I know, the above thing is a lot of code, but let's run a quick analysis and thought experiment on how every line just makes sense:

1. Most of our application will have the same **<head>** information. The meta tags rarely change and there are definitely CSS files and styles that we would like to apply for all of our pages, however, we will most likely want to distribute different css files to different pages in our website, so a css block completely makes sense there.

2. The header will most likely appear on all our pages, however, there are cases when we want our header to disappear, or appear completely differently (maybe on a marketing page). For this case, we allow an override on the entire header. Same goes for the footer.

3. The content block is essentially what you will always want to override in your pages.

4. At the end of the page, we will have the loaded javascript files. If we need more, we just add them to the override block on our page and we are done with that as well.

As a simple example, we are going to create a view and a template that displays information about the pizzas that we return in the view.

Listing 2-13. Pizza shuffling endpoint

```python
from django.shortcuts import render
from django.views import View

from pizza.models import Pizza

class GetTenPizzasView(View):
    template_name = 'ten_pizzas.html'

    def get(self, request)
        pizzas = Pizza.objects.order_by('?')[:10]
        return render(request, self.template_name, {'pizzas':
        pizzas})
```

The above code is a bit clumsy, but it will do the job of returning 10 random pizzas for us for now. Let's take a look at the template that we are going to build:

Listing 2-14. Pizza shuffling template

```
{# pizza/templates/ten_pizzas.html #}
{% extends 'base.html' %}

{% block content %}
<h2>Look at all the pizzas!</h2>
```

```
<table>
<th>
    <td>Name</td>
    <td>Description</td>
</th>
{% for pizza in pizzas %}
<tr>
    <td>{{ pizza.title }}</td>
    <td>{{ pizza.description }}</td>
</tr>
{% endfor %}
</table>

{% endblock %}
```

Quite simple, but it will do the job. So here we see that we have the ten pizzas rendered in a table one after another displaying their name and description. In Django templates we have all sorts of controls, like for loops and conditionals. Remember, all these operations take up valuable server time, since everything is calculated there. This might be good for your web application regarding page rankings on search engines, however, it might give your customers a slow client side experience. If you want something faster feeling, I might recommend relying entirely on Javascript and keeping your templates to as thin as possible.

For further reading on templates, I recommend checking out the documentation.

Permissions

When you're writing an application, you always need to make sure that entities can only be viewed, edited and removed by users who have the rights to do that. Again, we are lucky to have chosen Django as our tool for building **tizza**, since there's a built-in permission system at our hands already. If you're already familiar with UNIX based permissions, you can probably skip the next few paragraphs and jump into the code examples, for the rest of us, here's a primer on the terminology:

> **User** - We've already encountered users, they come from the **django.contrib.auth.models.User** model and describe a person (or a registration) in our system.

> **Group** - A group describes a group of users. One user can be part of many groups and one group can contain many users. Originates from **django.contrib. auth.models.Group**. Groups are an easy way of labeling your users. One possible use-case would be that in the tizza application we would like to restrict restaurant owners from updating their recipes due to maintenance in our caches. In this case, we can just take away the **restaurant_admin_page** rights from all users in the restaurant_owners group.

> **Permission** - Permission objects exist in the Django ecosystem physically as well, not just as tags. Using the **django.contrib.auth.models.Permission** class, you can create permission objects in the database itself.

User objects have the following two fields that could come in handy when working with permissions and groups:

- **user.groups** - You can fetch, set, add, remove and clear groups of a user through this field.

- **user.user_permissions** - You can fetch, set, add, remove and clear single permissions of a single user through this field.

Let's take a look at a quick example for permissions:

Listing 2-15. Permissions example

```python
# pizza/views.py
from django.contrib.auth.models import Permission

def index(request, pid):
    # ...
    elif request.method == 'DELETE':
        if 'can_delete' in request.user.user_permissions:
            pizza = Pizza.objects.get(id=pid)
            pizza.delete()
            return HttpResponse(
                content={
                    'id': pizza.id,
                }
            )
        else:
            return HttpResponse(status_code=404)
```

In the simple example above, we are checking if the user has permission to delete a given pizza. We can give this permission when they have created this pizza, or if they join the group that has permissions to work on it.

Conclusion

We've done a lot so far with the tizza application and there's still a long way to go for the finished product to be ready. For now we are going to leave it here. I've added Exercises 2-7 through 2-9 for the eager ones. If you just want to see the project in action, you can visit the following repository, clone the code base, and try out the application:

```
https://github.com/akoskaaa/dmswd-monolith
```

Even though the code base is still just a couple of thousand lines, we can already see that there might be certain areas in the project that might be better off on their own. In the next chapter, we are going to explore the options that we have to shard the project into smaller pieces and get familiarized with the principles that we are going to follow in the rest of the book.

If you need more learning material after this chapter, For more information, I highly recommend checking out the official Django website (`https://djangoproject.com`), as they have fantastic documentation and materials for both beginners and advanced users. There is also another excellent resource by Two Scoops Press (`https://www.twoscoopspress.com/`) where you can dive deeper into the topic.

EXERCISE 2-7: PIZZAS PAGE

It's very nice that we've created APIs for the models that we are working with, however, most of our users are not entirely familiar with the wonders of curl. For these people, let's create a page where we fetch the random pizzas, display them each one-by-one and offer them to either like or dislike them. When we are out of pizzas (or better: close to being out), let's fetch the next batch.

EXERCISE 2-8: RESTAURANT DASHBOARD

If you've worked with or used an e-commerce application before, you know that there are 2 types of users. People who buy (customers) and people who sell (merchants). So far we've mostly catered for the use case of the customers, let's make sure that the merchants get some love as well. For the users who have a pizzeria, they should receive a dashboard page where they can manage all the pizzas that they'd like to display in our system (create new ones, update and delete existing ones).

EXERCISE 2-9: PAYMENTS SERVICE

We need to start making money. Create a new application that will simulate payments for us from the merchant side, so they can "boost" the visibility of their products from their admin page.

CHAPTER 3

Anatomy of a Microservice

Now that we have a vague idea of what a microservice looks like from a birds eye view, it is time for us to zoom in and take a look at a closer anatomy of various services and how they interact with each other internally. For an easy understanding of our architecture, we are going to focus on 3 major categories, so reasoning is a bit easier when talking about the entire system

Firstly, we are going to look at the dimension on where in your architecture a specific service can be located. We are going to examine 3 types:

- Frontend services

- Mixed services

- Backend services

Let's start from what users don't see. You will see why.

Backend Services

Every system has components which the users don't really interact with directly, just through some many many layers of abstractions. You can, for example, imagine a state machine that calculates how the user is

© Akos Hochrein 2019
A. Hochrein, *Designing Microservices with Django*,
https://doi.org/10.1007/978-1-4842-5358-8_3

represented in the current system. Are they a former customer, or are they currently active? Perhaps they have never ever used a paying feature on your website before, yet for marketing purposes it is important to store their data.

Backend services are there to provide the backbone of your application. Most of these encapsulate functionalities that have the core business logic for the company. They oftentimes provide data or have something to do with data transformations. They are more likely to be providers of data to other services than consumers of it.

Designing pure backend applications sometimes feels like a trivial challenge and we will go over a couple of examples from our pizza application to make sure that we understand what this means. In Figure 3-1 you can see the pizza microservice connected to a data store that contains the models we have defined in the previous chapter under the pizza Django application.

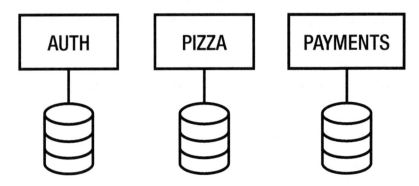

Figure 3-1. *The tizza application backend systems imagined*

Well, at least some of them, as we will see in a couple of chapters. Another service that you can see on the diagram is the auth service, this we will use for all user related information and authentication. Some teams also use a service like auth for authorization, depending on your taste, you can move that layer to a separate part of your architecture as well. Keep in mind, though, that data that exists in similar or the same business domain often should stay close.

One thing that is definitely worth mentioning here is that the design of these services is driven by both the data that they host and the domain that they work in. It is a very common mistake when building microservices to create services that are only there to host a single specific data type. When different types of data lie in similar business domains, they should live close to each other physically and logically. This is, however, always a tough call to make. Here are a couple of cases that you can lament over with your colleagues during lunch break:

- Should pizzas and pizzerias be hosted on the same service in the same data store or not? What if we start storing topping for pizzas? Would your opinion change in that case?

- Where should we store permissions? Should it be bound to the pizzas or bound to the users of our system?

- Where should we store likes?

There are multiple good answers to all of the questions above. My recommendation is to think of it this way: if the data is not or loosely coupled, then you're safe to break it up. If it's tightly coupled, try to measure how tight the coupling is. You can always measure, for example, how many times do you query the different resources together from your data store, it might help you make the decision.

Keeping all the data in the same place can work for some time for your company. As a matter of fact, keeping data in the same place will speed up your operations significantly in the beginning. However, after a while, the issues and stories that we mentioned in chapter 1 will come up again and again. It's a real shame if you have a single table in your database that is not very critical but fills up your storage and causes an outage to your core business. On the other hand, moving everything apart will remove your ability to create joins and fast operations that happen on the storage level, you will need to fetch data from different sources and connect them manually, sometimes writing inefficient queries.

Some of this talk might give you an idea of doing data duplication amongst your various storages. Let's do a quick detour around this topic.

A Note on Data Duplication

Now that we've talked a lot about how the data serving services work, I'd like to take a short detour to talk about data duplication between the different data stores that you're going to be working with when you migrate to microservices.

Data duplication can come very naturally when working with microservices. After all, you _do_ need the email address in your service, right? Why not store it when the user was created and then you can be confident that this data is available to you at all times.

Thinking like this can be very deceptive. When you're working with microservices (and really, anything in software), the one thing that you always want to reduce, is maintenance work. When you introduce a new database, table or even just a field in your service, you're creating ownership and maintenance work for yourself. In the email example mentioned above, you need to make sure that the email always stays up-to-date, meaning that you got to make sure that if your user changes it in the auth service, you need to change it as well in your own! When the customer wants to use their right to be forgotten, you need to make sure that you remove or anonymize the email address in your data store as well. On the long run this can cause a lot of inconsistencies and headaches.

Keeping data consistent across many systems is a very difficult problem. Database engineers have been fighting the CAP theorem for decades, creating algorithms like the hinted handoff or the Sloppy Quorum, achieving eventual consistency across various database replicas. Is it worth implementing complex consistency algorithms like these in your application?

As you can tell, I am not a huge fan of data duplication. Naturally, there are situations where you cannot avoid it, however, I usually recommend the following alternatives:

- Virtual objects: Why do you need to store the entire user object if you can store an identifier with which you can query that object from another system?

- Client and server side caching: Think about the data you're working with. How important is it to be up-to-date? The owner service of the data can always implement a caching layer easily, but the same can happen on the client side as well!

Think about alternatives before you start copying data from other services. It might cost you dearly in the long run.

Now that we have a good understanding of where and how our data will be stored, let's take a look at service types that will consume them.

Front-end Services

Frontend services exist to containerize the front-end applications rendered on the users' machines. At first glance their existence might not make a lot of sense, however, there are a couple of reasons why designing services that are (almost) fully frontend might make sense for you and your teams:

- Separation of concern - you might remember (or still work with) MVC models and the benefits of them separating the various parts of your application. In a way, you can think about frontend services as the "view" layer of your MVC. Developers can specialize into working with these services, only utilizing interfaces of others and interacting with data that they are not owners of.

53

- Separate tooling - if there are different teams working on front-end services, there will be different tooling around it as well with more specialized people for this field. Not all people who are familiar with gradle are familiar with Webpack. However, this doesn't necessarily mean that they cannot learn from each other!

Front-end services can consume data directly from backend services and systems that are there to integrate the data provided by the backend services into a more digestible format defined by specific business logic. Let's take a look at mixed services.

Mixed Services

As per the philosophy of SoA, sometimes we need systems that do just one thing for our business and it does that right. Engineers who have no specialization in frontend or backend need to take care of these services. It is also entirely possible that these business components don't tie to the engineering department strictly. The main focus of this book will be around backend and mixed services.

If ownership or lack of people to maintain systems dictates, we can completely consider systems, that I like to call "mixed services". In the wild, they are sometimes referred to as backend to frontend services, or BFFs.

Mixed services have plenty of frontend and backend components wired together to achieve a simple business goal. Let's take a look at an example before we jump into the code:

Let's imagine a world, where in a distant future, we become the technical leads of one of the most important teams in tizza, which is the tizza-admin team. Our mission is to make sure that all pizza creators can easily manage their pizzas and can promote marketing campaigns inside the application itself. They need a single page app for this to make the experience smooth. After reading the specification, the following questions might arise:

1. There's a lot of data going on here, where should we get if from?

2. Should we call all service endpoints separately from the frontend?

3. What about mobile? Can they handle all the data?

All of these are valid questions that every full-stack (and non-thereof) should ask themselves when building single page applications with multiple data sources. The first thing that we won't want to do is connect to the existing databases (we will have more reasoning about this later in the chapter), so we will confine ourselves to calling APIs. Here we have the option of calling the endpoints of our data (in this case, for example we need the list of pizzas, the permissions, campaign options and payment details, amongst many other things) from separate data sources or from a single one. With the power of event loops and threads, we can easily run the first option to parallelly get all the information at the same time, however, we are using up a lot of network bandwidth.

Why is this an important question? In 2017, 63% of all network traffic in the United States was done via mobile devices, a lot of this through mobile networks. Mobile networks are fickle little beings. They are flaky, weak, the roundtrip-time is abysmal and people take them to places where the Sun only rarely shines, which makes network bandwidth optimization one of the top priorities we need to consider as engineers.

Changing the currently existing endpoints to support partial response payloads might be a bit of a hassle, so here comes the idea of a service that would aggregate the data for us and respond in a compact response. The drawback? We have introduced an extra call to the BFF.

With the separate service comes another beautiful thing, which is ownership. BFFs are usually the parts of your system which have the most business logic in it, making it the perfect candidate for ownership of product teams.

Now that we are familiar with the basic concepts of how we categorize microservices, we are going to do a dive into how a high level architecture of a service is supposed to look like.

Design Principles

We are going to take a look at methodologies like the SOLID principles - which are originally used with monolithic services to manage code complexity - and how they provide a useful way of thinking about services. We are also going to take a look at a couple of common design patterns that emerge during service design.

Keep in mind that the examples that we are to look at in this part should be taken with a grain of salt and thinking. These are not patterns that will solve all difficulties when designing services. Keep an open mind during your implementation and focus on your business problems when integrating these principles into your systems.

SOLID Building Blocks

Some of you might have heard about the SOLID principles formulated by legendary software engineers, like Sandi Metz and Robert C. Martin, if not, this might be a very eye-opening little snippet here.

The SOLID principles are essentially guidelines on how to design your code and code architecture to spend the least amount of time with feature development and maintenance in the future. We will briefly go through the 5 principles with some examples. If you'd like to read more about it, I highly recommend Clean Architecture by Robert C. Martin as reading material. These principles are not strictly related to microservice design, but I've found a great deal of inspiration in them while thinking about the systems that me and my team was building. Also, understanding and applying them (if needed) will objectively make you a better programmer.

1. Single responsibility principle - States that a member of your system (class, method, or even an entire microservice!) should only have a single reason to change. What does this mean? Think about a function that is responsible for fetching data from a data storage and displaying it on a web UI. Now, this component might have 2 reasons to change. First, if the data or the datastore changes that it reads from, like adding a new column to a database table. Second, if the format that it displays the data changes, like allowing `json` formats as well as `xml` data as your response. Ideally, you'd like to keep these layers separate. Since they become easier to reason about.

2. Open-close principle - States that parts of your system should be open to extension, but closed to modification. Now, this doesn't mean that you should write code that is impossible to change and fix in the future, rather it means that if you'd like to add new functionality to your software, you should not need to change the already existing code to do so.

Listing 3-1. Not conforming to open-close

```
def pizzas(request):
    if request.method != 'GET':
        # we are post (I guess)
        return update_pizzas(request)
    else:
        return get_pizzas(request)
```

Adding a new method type to the above code requires serious modifications

Listing 3-2. Still not conforming to open-close

```
def pizzas(request):
    if request.method != 'GET' and request.method != 'PUT':
        # still post! (I guess)
        return update_pizzas(request)
    elif request.method == 'PUT':
        return create_pizzas(request)
    else:
        return get_pizzas(request)
```

Instead, consider the following (still not the best, but will suffice):

Listing 3-3. Conforming to the open-close

```
PIZZA_METHOD_ROUTER = {
    'GET': get_pizzas,
    'PUT': create_pizzas,
    'POST': update_pizzas,
}

def pizzas(request):
    return PIZZA_METHOD_ROUTER.get(request.method)()
```

3. Liskov substitution principle - States that if you have types in your program that has subtypes, the instances of said type should be replaceable by the subtypes without breaking your program. One of the more object oriented principles of the 5, this essentially states that if your abstractions of your code should be replaceable by the concrete members if required, this way ensuring correctness of the system in the long run. I found that the Liskov substitution principle is quite easy to follow if the engineer uses an IDE that tells them if they are breaking the rules of the superclass. One additional thing that makes it much easier to follow this principle is to minimize the use of metaprogramming. This we will get into later in the book.

4. Interface segregation principle - States that many client-specific interfaces are better than a few big abstract ones that have many functionalities. In other words, you don't want your clients to depend on things that they don't need. This is a very-very important principle in modern software engineering that is many times ignored. Basically the idea behind the service oriented architecture principles.

Imagine that you're a backend developer. Your job is to write pristine, multi purpose APIs that hundreds of internal and external clients use every single minute. Your interfaces have grown throughout the years into massive monsters, some of them have no limits of the amount of data they return about the customer. From the first name to the number of restaurants they've attended with the list of friends for each visit is returned in the response every single time. Now, it's possible that it's easy for you, the database is sitting beneath you and with clever queries on your MySQL cluster, you were able to keep the APIs blazing fast. However, the mobile teams suddenly start complaining. They are saying that you cannot possibly expect customers to download hundreds of kilobytes of data each time they open the application! It is true, the massive APIs would definitely be better off sharded into smaller ones. This way the data that is queried is more specific and the refactoring and extension of such backend services will be faster. When building APIs, always start from the client!

5. Dependency inversion principle - States that systems should depend upon abstractions, not concretions. Probably one of the most famous ones from the 5. Basically states that you should be using clearly defined interfaces in your code and your components should be depending on these. This way, you give yourself flexibility in the implementation layer.

Microservices are - supposed to be - all about the dependency inversion principle. In an ideal world the systems communicate using contracts, such as API definitions to make sure that every service is on the same page about what sort of data is produced and can be consumed. Sadly, the real world is not always littered with such sunshine and happiness, but we are going to take a look at methodologies on how we can aspire for this.

One thing that people often forget about microservice design is that it does not permit you to write bad code and follow bad design patterns on the low level. Make sure that you're proud of the system that you design both on low and high levels of abstraction, and that this service is not just replaceable, but maintainable as well.

12 factors

One of the more popular service design methodologies is following the rules of the 12 factor app. Originally authored by Adam Wiggins and later on forked and maintained by Heroku, the 12 factor app is a microservice design methodology collection that gives us 12 points that should be followed to build a scalable and maintainable service. Now, these methodologies cover a much wider spectrum than what this cook can cover in-dept, so I recommend reading more at 12factor.net.

1. There should be one codebase tracked in the revision control system, deployed multiple times

I think nowadays there are not too many codebases that are not tracked with various revision systems, such as Git or Subversion. If you're one of the people who have not adapted these technologies, I heavily recommend checking them out and integrating them into your workflow. An app should consist of one codebase with one or more deployments. In object oriented terms you can think of your codebase being a class and a deployment an instance of your class with various parameters that enable it to run in production, development or test environments.

Your codebase can have different versions in different deployments. For example, your local development deployment can be running on a different version of the codebase as you are building the application.

2. Dependencies should be isolated and explicitly declared

As we are going to learn from later parts of the book, dependency management is one of the biggest and most difficult questions of building microservices. The second rule of the 12 can give us a couple of rule of thumb that we can follow to get started.

In the python world we usually use pip combined with requirements or setup files as a dependency managers. This rule dictates that all your dependencies should have pinned versions. What does this mean? Imagine the following situation: you're using package A in your application with an unpinned version. Everything goes completely fine until a critical security gets found in the package and you never get notified of it. Furthermore, the only maintainer of the project has disappeared 8 months ago, leaving all your user data stolen. Now, this might sound like an extreme situation, but if you've ever worked with dependency managers like **npm** and the version indicators like ^ and ~ you know what I am talking about. Stay on the safe side and use == for your dependencies.

3. Store configurations in the environment

In order to adhere to rule #1, we need to store the deployment dependent configurations separately from the deployment itself. Deployment dependent configurations could be many things and they are often essential for your application to run. We are referencing to variables such as:

- Database and other external system's URIs

- Credentials

- Settings for logging and monitoring

4. Treat external services as resources

External services can vary from databases and caches to mail services or even completely internal applications that provide some sort of service to your application. These systems need to be treated as resources, meaning that your application should support changing their origin on demand. The application should make no difference between third party environments.

Imagine the following situation: there is a massive marketing campaign coming up and your third-party email provider just cannot take the load. Upgrading your plan might take some time, but spinning up a new (higher throughput plan) application in the third party seems like a viable and quick solution. A 12 factor app should be able to handle the switch without much issues, as it doesn't care about the environment it's sitting in, only the configuration it's using. In the example, changing the auth credentials of the application saved the day.

5. *The non-development deployment creation should support the build - release - run cycle*

A 12 factor app separates deployment creation into 3 separate stages

- Build - When your code and dependencies are assembled into an executable.

- Release - When your assembled executable gets combined with the environmental configs and creates a release ready for execution in a given environment.

- Run - The assembled executable and configs now run in the given environment.

Why is it so important that we shard this process? It's a very good question, and the most simple answer I can give is reasoning about the application. Imagine the following: there is a critical bug in production for your payment systems. The team immediately starts looking at application code on your version management system, checking the most recent commits while the revert was happening. Nothing had indicated that the issue should've happened in the first place, still the team made the decision not to re-release the broken version until the bug is found. Only days later the team learned that an engineer made changes to the production code for the payments systems. This is one of the examples that the 12 factor applications would like to avoid with this rule.

Now, the above problem is quite difficult to solve without proper security restrictions to your production systems, however, there are tools to discourage engineers from doing this in the first place. For instance, you can use a proper release management system, where rollbacks of applications are simple, such as `helm` for Kubernetes. In addition, all of your releases should have a version and a timestamp attached, preferably stored in a changelog (we are going to dive deeper into these sort of systems in later chapters).

6. 12 factor apps are stateless processes

12 factor applications assume that nothing will be stored long term on the disk or in memory next to the main application. The reason for this is, again, being able to reason about the application and the bugs it might be associated with in the future. Naturally, this doesn't mean that you cannot use the memory, it is recommended to think of it as a single request cache. If you store many things in-memory and your process restarts for some reason (such as a new deployment), you will lose all that data, which might not be beneficial to your business.

Applications with persistent sessions, where user data could be reused multiple times across requests, should still be stored in some sort of data store, in this case this can be a cache. Later in the book we are going to explore some python packages and frameworks, like **asyncio** and **aiohttp-jobs** where it's very easy to enter the danger-zone of storing your requests in memory and losing it altogether during a process restart.

7. Export your services using port-binding

A little bit more web-development specific (but hey, most of this book is about that), this rule dictates that the application should be entirely self contained, should not depend on the runtime injection of a web server, but exports it's interfaces by binding to a port and serving requests through there.

In our cases, Django will take care of all of this.

8. Scale out using processes

The base of every application should be the process, which should be interpreted as Unix-like service daemons. Various types of processes should be designed to handle various types of payload. Longer running tasks with heavier computation might require workers or other asynchronous processes, whereas HTTP requests might require web processes to handle.

This doesn't mean that threads are discouraged from the runtime of your process, in case of Python, your application can absolutely utilize the `threading` library, or `asyncio`. On the other hand, your application needs to be able to expand as multiple processes running on the same or multiple physical and/or virtual machines.

Make sure to not overcomplicate things on the operation system level, just use the standard tools for managing your processes, like `systemd` or `supervisor`.

Point number 6 enables this.

9. Processes should be easy to spin up and dispose of

Have not attachment to the processes of your 12 factor apps, as they should be just as easy to get rid of, as easy they are to create. At a moments notice. This comes with a couple of requirements though.

- Startup should be fast - processes should take just a few seconds to start up. This is needed for simplified scaling and fast release process. Achieving this can be quite tricky. You should make sure that there are no expensive operations when you're loading your application - such as remote calls to separate web servers. If you're using many modules, you might want to look into the **lazy_import** method of **importlib**.

- Shutdown should be graceful - when your process receives a **SIGINT** (or even **SIGTERM**) from the operating system, it should make sure that everything shuts down in order, meaning that the running process/request finishes in your application, the network connections and the file handlers are closed. In the case of django, the selected WSGI servers are going to take care of this for you.

10. Keep development and production as close as possible

Make sure that the code that's running in production is as close to the code running on the development machines is as close as possible. Just for the sake of avoiding a misunderstanding, by closeness, we mean the difference between the version of the application running. According to the 12 factor app, you will need to work on 3 "gaps" to achieve this:

- Time: The actual time that takes the developer to deliver a feature to production - Whether this is days or weeks for you and your company currently, the goal is to reduce it to hours or even minutes.

- Personnel: The time it takes for the ops engineer to deploy the code - Developers of 12 factor apps should be able to be involved in the deployment process and monitor the application without the need of an ops engineer.

- Tools: The tools that are used during development versus the tools that are being used in production (i.e. databases, remote systems, etc.) - Keep the development and production tooling as close as possible.

You might think that most of these are easier said than done. A decade ago it was almost impossible to imagine services being deployed without ops people in place in the matter of minutes. Most continuous development and deployment systems were built by hand using various collected scripts from the ops people who had gotten bored of running `rsync`s every time someone changed something in the codebase. Today there are entire industries and technology branches developed to make the deployment experience faster, simpler and less error prone. There are systems which can just hook up to your git repository and offer automated deployments to your clusters, such as AWS CodePipeline, CircleCI or Jenkins.

Note   If you're not familiar with continuous integration (CI) or continuous deployment (CD) pipelines, I recommend doing some reading on it. There are excellent resources found on devops.com.

Regarding the tooling, today, in the age of containerization, there are multiple tools that you and your developers can use to simplify this. Before we take a glance at them, let's take a look at why this is important:

Imagine the following situation: a developer of yours is working on a very complicated query that your system's ORM cannot handle, so you decide to use a RAW query for the solution. The developer fires up their local systems and started building the query on their local SQLite database. After a couple of days, the multi-hundred line query is complete, covered with automated and manual tests, everything works like a charm. The developer gets that approvals on their pull-request, and after deployment your monitoring system alerts the team that the feature is not operational. After some debugging, the developer comes to the conclusion that there was a syntax difference between his local SQLite database and the Postgres running in production that he hadn't known of.

In the past it made sense to run lightweight backing services on your local development deploy, since the resources on your machine were usually limited and expensive. Today with the monster development machines that we use this is no longer an issue. The other problem could be the availability of the type of backend services. Maintaining a

Postgres cluster on your local machine might seem tedious, and it is, if you don't have the tooling backup that is provided today with the power of virtualization and especially containerization.

Setting up a Postgres database on your local machine is as easy today as writing a Docker compose file that looks something like this:

Listing 3-4. Sample yaml to spin up a database with Docker Compose

```
version: '3'
services:
  postgres:
    image: postgres:11.6.1
    ports:
      - "5432:5432"
```

There are no more excuses! Make sure to use a similar ecosystem in all your deploys, to reduce the type of errors detailed above.

11. Logs should be managed by something else

This point is quite simple. A 12 factor app should not concern itself with managing and writing to various loglines and should treat all logs as an event stream that is written to `stdout`. This makes development quite easy, since on the local machine the developer can see what events are happening in their application, speeding up the debug process.

In staging and production environments, the streams are collected by the execution environment, and then shipped for viewing and/or archival. These destinations should not be configurable by the 12 factor application.

Nowadays there are dozens of great logging solutions at your disposal. If you are unsure where to start, I recommend checking out Logstash, Graylog or Flume.

12. Run your administrative processes as one-off processes

Oftentimes developers need to run manual processes/scripts for maintenance purposes on the 12 factor app. Some examples include:

- **manage.py migrate** for database migrations on your Django application

- One time scripts to patch user data in the database

- **manage.py shell** for getting a Python shell to inspect the application state versus the database

These processes should be run in an identical environment as where the long running processes of the app are running. They require the same codebase and the same configurations. Admin code must ship with the application code to the various environments.

Conclusion

Now that we went through the rules of the 12 factor application, we might have a vague idea what a performant microservice looks like. Ideally, you have heard of most of these points and think of them as things that would be worthy additions to your arsenal of designing services. There will be some parts of this book, where we are going to observe how these rules can be broken in ways which might be considered acceptable, due to the development or business constraints you have. Wherever we will break the rules of the 12 factor, I will let you know and you can evaluate yourself if it's worth it or not.

We've embraced a couple of high level design philosophies about how our services should look like from a bird's eye view. Now we are going to zoom in and learn how they should communicate with each other.

CHAPTER 4

Communication

So we already have a good basic idea on what microservices look like and how we can conceptually start creating them. In this chapter we are going to dig a little bit deeper into the topic of how these services can, should and will interact with each other. We are going to cover topics of synchronous and asynchronous communication, security and testing. Fasten your seatbelts and let's jump straight into the basics of REST.

REST and the Synchronous World

Back in the heroic ages, there were no real high level definitions of what communication meant on the internet. You might remember attending networking classes where you learned about TCP and UDP protocols, all the thing about the ACK and NACK cycles and various handshakes that happen to make sure that you can connect to different systems. Hell, you might have even coded a remote calculator in C where you used sockets to talk to different open ports on your machine. Oh, those were the days!

Truly, we are lucky that higher level standardization has started a couple of decades ago and has not stopped since. The first protocol we are going to focus on is the HTTP and HTTPS protocols and we are going to examine best practices through REST that you can follow to create concise and synchronous communication between your services.

REST stands for REpresentational State Transfer. It is a protocol that was first coined in the legendary dissertation of Roy Thomas Fielding in

© Akos Hochrein 2019
A. Hochrein, *Designing Microservices with Django*,
https://doi.org/10.1007/978-1-4842-5358-8_4

the year 2000, called Architectural Styles and the Design of Network-based Software Architectures. Without going into too much detail regarding the paper, it describes methodologies and terminologies of system design in the 90s, forging a solid ground of best practices that still last today. It's definitely a mandatory read for everyone who wants to do serious system design. The REST protocol was detailed in the 5th chapter of the paper.

What is REST

REST, as was mentioned before is a messaging protocol that was designed to allow stateless communication between various services on the web, stateless communication meaning that messages that a receiver receives do not matter on previous messages. Services that adhere to the REST principles allow modification of resources and entities through textual representation in the request.

If this sounds a little bit out of whack take a look at one of the **tizza** APIs in Listing 4-1.

Listing 4-1. Example restful pizza API

```
def pizzas(request, pid):
    if request.method == 'PUT':
        data = request.json()
        pizza = Pizza.objects.create(**data)
        return HttpResponse(status_code=201, data={
            'id': pizza.id,
        })
    else:
        return HttpResponse(status_code=405)
```

In the above example, we can see a view function that either creates a pizza or returns a weird status code to the caller of the API. You can see that we've used a HTTP verb, PUT to check the operation. This is one of the standards that REST gives us. Depending on the verb you're using, you should be doing certain operations in your application, so the caller of the API can know what to expect. The status code that we've used in the response is a 201, which stands for "created". The status codes are similar to the verbs. If we see a 201, we know what to expect as a caller. 405 stands for method not supported. In listing 4-2, you can see an example representation of a HTTP response of a not found resource.

Listing 4-2. Example HTTP response

```
$ curl -v -X GET localhost:8000/pizzas/101
Note: Unnecessary use of -X or --request, GET is already
inferred.
*   Trying 127.0.0.1...
* TCP_NODELAY set
* Connected to localhost (127.0.0.1) port 8000 (#0)
> GET /pizzas/101 HTTP/1.1
> Host: localhost:8000
> User-Agent: curl/7.54.0
> Accept: */*
>
< HTTP/1.1 404 Not Found
< Date: Sat, 21 Sep 2019 14:13:07 GMT
< Server: WSGIServer/0.2 CPython/3.6.5
< Content-Type: text/html
< X-Frame-Options: SAMEORIGIN
< Content-Length: 3405
<
...
```

These standards might seem like a burden when you're designing services and communication, but they will make your application much more usable and can reduce unnecessary interaction between the engineers in your company in the long run. Now, let's take a look at how REST works.

HTTP Verbs, the Way REST Talks

Let's go through the HTTP verbs list so we get a common understanding of what I mean when I am talking about HTTP verbs:

GET - Get is probably the most common HTTP verb used today on the internet, being the default one that you use when you visit a website on your browser. All it does is, well, it gets a resource from the endpoint that is specified. If you're developing and API that serves an endpoint with a GET verb, one of the expectations of you callee is going to be that the service acting as the endpoint does not modify the server side state of the application (such as writing to it's database), meaning that a GET should always be idempotent. Here's an example of what we'd like to avoid:

```
$ curl -X GET localhost:8000/pizzas/1
{"id": 1, "title": "Pepperoni and Cheese", "description":
"Yumm"}
$ curl -X GET localhost:8000/pizzas/1
{"id": 1, "title": "Salami Picante", "description":
"Also YUMM"}
```

What happened here? We called the endpoint twice and it didn't return the same response. Now, arguable in some cases, this might be the expected result, such as returning a random response on the endpoint or the resource being modified in-between requests, however, not if the GET endpoint does like in Listing 4-3:

Listing 4-3. A view that changes the data on GET

```python
from django.http import JsonResponse

from pizza.models import Pizza

def get_pizza(request, pid):
    if request.method == 'GET':
        pizza = Pizza.objects.get(id=pid)
        pizza.title = 'Salami Picante'
        pizza.description = 'Also YUMM'
        pizza.save()
        return JsonResponse(
            data={
                'id': pizza.id,
                'title': pizza.title,
                'description': pizza.description,
            }
        )
```

If we want to keep idempotency, we don't do the above code. Now, before we get into too many philosophical arguments over what application state means, in the context of this book, we are going to call the objects that are directly accessed through the APIs application state.

Note   In the above curl, I've used the -X GET flags, normally this is not required when you're doing a GET request with curl.

PUT - One of the other important HTTP verbs. PUT represents the replacement or creation of an object that is sent in the payload of the request. The object identifier is often represented in the URI of the request itself, and the body contains the members that need to be overwritten in the system. PUT requests are supposed to be idempotent by nature. Meaning:

```
$ curl -i -X PUT localhost:8000/pizzas/1 -d '{"title":
"Diavola", "description": "Spicy!"}'
HTTP/1.1 201 Created
```

...

```
{"id": 1, "title": "Diavola", "description": "Spicy!"}
$ curl -i -X PUT localhost:8000/pizzas/1 -d '{"title":
"Pikante", "description": "Spicy!"}'
HTTP/1.1 200 OK
```

...

```
{"id": 1, "title": "Pikante", "description": "Spicy!"}
```

So, no matter what happened, we always got back the same object, with the same identifier.

POST - Oftentimes confused with PATCH, POST is the non-idempotent counterpart. Meaning that every time you send a POST request to your resource's endpoint, you should always expect a new resource to be created there.

```
$ curl -i -X POST localhost:8000/pizzas/ -d '{"title":
"Diavola", "description": "Spicy!"}'
HTTP/1.1 201 Created
```

...

```
{"id": 1, "title": "Diavola", "description": "Spicy!"}
$ curl -i -X POST localhost:8000/pizzas/ -d '{"title":
"Diavola", "description": "Spicy!"}'
HTTP/1.1 200 OK
```

...

```
{"id": 2, "title": "Diavola", "description": "Spicy!"}
```

You can also see that in the above curls that we are not specifying the identifier of the object we'd like to be working with.

PATCH - What the difference between PUT, POST and PATCH is a notoriously popular interview question on web developer interviews. Now that we know that PUT is supposed to create and replace the object specified in the URL and POST is there to create new objects in the remote system, we can deduct that PATCH requests are there to make modifications on an already existing resource. If the resource doesn't exist, then the response should announce this to us. Meaning that PATCH is not an idempotent HTTP verb.

```
$ curl -i -X PATCH localhost:8000/pizzas/2 -d '{"title":
"Diavola", "description": "Spicy!"}'
HTTP/1.1 404 Not Found
...
$ curl -i -X POST localhost:8000/pizzas/1 -d '{"title":
"Diavola", "description": "Spicy!"}'
HTTP/1.1 200 OK
...

{"id": 1, "title": "Diavola", "description": "Spicy!"}
```

DELETE - One of the easier verbs, it is there to note that we would like to eliminate a specific resource from the system.

There are a couple of less-popular HTTP verbs that we will quickly take a glance at:

HEAD - This verb is used to get only the headers of a request before issuing a proper GET request. This might come in handy if you're uncertain about the content type or the size of the response that you'd need to process and it can give your systems an educated decision to actually make the request or not.

OPTIONS - With this HTTP verb, you can figure out what other HTTP verbs are accepted on the given resource.

Response Codes, What REST Really Means When it's Talking

After taking this look at the HTTP verbs, we will take a quick glance at the most popular response codes as well. Response codes are essentially how REST communicates how a request was processed in the system we are sending it to. Let's take a look at some examples above.

```
$ curl -i -X POST localhost:8000/pizzas/ -d '{"title":
"Diavola", "description": "Spicy!"}'
HTTP/1.1 201 Created
```

With this POST request, we wanted to ensure that there's a Diavola pizza exists with the description of "spicy!" in the tizza backends. The response can be decomposed in the following way:

HTTP/1.1 - HTTP version, tells us what HTTP version was used for the request-response cycle itself. Normally we don't really need to care for this, however, there are older systems which don't support version 1.1 and there are some newer systems which already support 2.0. In most cases we don't need to worry about this.

201 - Response code, which is a numerical representative of what happened in the system we've sent the request to. Oftentimes you will need to write logic to handle the response of an external system according to the response code, see Listing 4-4 below.

Listing 4-4. Example response status code handling

```
import requests

...
response = requests.get('pizza/1')
if 404 == response.status_code:
    # We couldn't find the pizza, panic!
    ...
...
```

Note   Above, we are using the **requests** library to make an HTTP request from one system to another. For beginner Python users, I highly recommend reading the documentation on 3.python-requests.org. Also, take a look at the source code on Github, as it is one of the most well written Python packages out there.

Created - HTTP status verb. This is essentially the written form of the status code. Programatically it is a bit troublesome to process, thus we usually ignore it when we are processing responses and rely on the status code.

After this simple example, we now understand that response status codes are core members of RESTful communication. We are not going to go through all of them (as there are over 60), however, here's a list of them that I recommend to follow. For the rest of them, make sure to check out resources like Wikipedia or httpstatuses.com.

2xx status codes usually resemble acceptance and success.

200 OK - Hopefully the most common response status code you encounter, in general it indicates that your intent to the external system was successfully processed. This could mean anything from a resource was fetched from a data store to a resource was created.

201 Created - Normally I consider differentiating between various 200 responses a bit of a waste. Sometimes, however, it can be informative for the processing client to see what has happened in the external system. 201 and 202 are, to me, some of these informative messages that should be processed if required. 201 indicates that a new resource has been created in the external system. If you recall from a couple of pages back, we were checking out the PUT HTTP verb, where a resource can either be created, or updated. 201 can be a great differentiator for the client in this case.

202 Accepted - The accepted keyword will come in handy in the future. Basically it indicates that the request has been recorded in the

called system, however, there is no response just yet. This response code usually means that the request has entered a queueing system, which will eventually process it.

3xx response codes usually indicate that a resource has been moved to a different location.

301 Moved permanently - This status code indicates that the requested resource has been moved to a different URI. Oftentimes it brings a redirection with itself as well. The new URI should be located in the Location header parameter in this case. Many browsers do the redirection by default using that header.

304 Not modified - An exception in the 3xx family. This response code indicates by the server that the requested resource has not been modified, so the client can use whatever cached data it has on it. This is only true if the client has indicated that the request is conditional, meaning that it already has the mentioned data stored locally.

4xx responses indicate that there was an error on the client side when accessing the required resource. In these cases, the client should reconsider modifying the request before sending it again.

400 Bad request - Probably the most common response code in the 4xx family. Indicates that there was an error in the request itself. At this point it could mean data validation (for example having too long of a name for a pizza) or just a malformed request setting, like unsupported content type.

401 Unauthorized & 403 Forbidden - The access control duo. Usually indicates the lack of credentials or the lack of sufficient credentials to access a resource.

404 Not found - Indicates that a certain resource cannot be found in the called system. This response code is often used as a replacement for 401 and 403, if we want to hide the existence of the resource that we'd like to access, making it more secure, but more confusing for the client engineers.

429 Too many requests - Another important one from the 4xx family. This response code indicates that there were too many calls in a given time period to the resource holding system. We can also call this response

"rate limit reached." Retrying these requests could lead to catastrophic consequences, locking out systems for hours, depending on the resource holder's server implementation.

5xx responses indicate that there has been a failure on the server side. If you're a resource holder, you should receive alerts and measure the number of these responses in your system. Retrying these is reasonable on the client side.

500 Server error - The most common form of the 5xx family. Indicates that there was an unhandled (or handled, but not accounted for) exception on the server side. For resource owners, these exceptions should be logged and accounted for.

502 Bad gateway & 503 Service unavailable - The gateway or proxy before the server has received an invalid response from the server itself and has issues fulfilling the request. Could be due to the application server being unresponsive, in this case, make sure that all processes are properly running on the server side.

504 Gateway timeout - The gateway or proxy of your application server didn't receive a response in a timely manner. This could indicate various failures on the server side, starting from overwhelmed CPU and/or memory to a dead database connection pool.

These are the basic HTTP responses and verbs that I like using in my application. If you follow and respect these on both the client and the server side, I can guarantee that there will be less friction while developing software between your engineering teams and microservices. Let's look at a practice exercise for our tizza server.

Note   RESTful backends are oftentimes hand-written by humans, meaning that there's significant error-ratio involved. Most people have their own understanding of how REST should be working. Take the above section with a pinch of salt (and maybe some oregano as well) and make sure that when you're working with an external system, you are well versed in how it operates.

EXERCISE 4-1: RESTFUL PIZZAS

We've talked a lot about the status codes and the HTTP verbs. I'd like to ask you now to go back to the code you've written in chapter 2 and reevaluate it according to what we've learned so far in this chapter. What endpoints and resources follow the REST principles and which ones don't?

Now that we are familiar with REST, let's take a look at some tooling that Django offers us regarding this technology.

The Django REST Framework

I know what you're thinking. We've learned all these things about responses and making sure that our services can communicate with each other in a concise way through HTTP, this seems like an awful lot of work though. Luckily, Django has a drop-in solution to make your server side code RESTful in an instant. Let me introduce you to the Django REST Framework.

As a starter we will need to install the framework itself. In your virtual environment, run the following code:

```
pip install djangorestframework
```

The Django REST Framework needs to be registered as an application to your Django project. To do this, extend your **settings.py** file with the following:

```
INSTALLED_APPS = (
    ... # Here are the Django builtins
    'rest_framework',
    ... # Here are your custom apps
)
```

Voilais! Now you can use the Django REST framework at your pleasure. Let's hook it up to out ORM.

Serializers

First off, we are going to create a serializer. Serializers exist so we can transform our models that reside in our data store to something that is more REST-friendly and processable by other systems. What do I mean by this? When various systems are talking to each other, they need a common understanding on how the data that is being transferred should be represented. The raw models from the database could be transferred as well, however, it is unlikely that the consumer application will understand what that data actually means. For this, we need to convert the data into a common format, which in today's world is usually JSON. For this demonstration, we are going to use the default serializer provided by the framework, but you can easily write your own or use one from the Python package index.

Let's create a file in our pizza app called **serializers.py** in Listing 4-5.

Listing 4-5. Our pizza serializer

```
from rest_framework import serializers

from tizza.pizza.models import Pizza

class PizzaSerializer(serializers.HyperlinkedModelSerializer):

    class Meta:
        model = Pizza
        fields = ('id', 'title', 'description')
```

This declaration basically describes that if someone would want to access the pizza resource in the future, they will receive the id, the title and the description fields, automatically converted to the right format by the framework. As you can see, this is not the only job of the serializer. For example, you can also filter data here that you would like to send to the clients as responses, meaning that you can make sure that you don't publish sensitive, or server-specific data. We have converted our data into something that will be understandable by the client side, time to create a view for it.

View Sets

Our next step is to create something that we call a view set. This basically describes what type of query should run when we try to access the resource itself. Let's create a **viewsets.p**y file in our pizza application, see Listing 4-6.

Listing 4-6. The pizza viewset

```
from rest_framework import viewsets

from pizza.models import Pizza
from pizza.serializers import PizzaSerializer

class PizzaViewSet(viewsets.ModelViewSet):
    queryset = Pizza.objects.all()
    serializer_class = PizzaSerializer
```

The code looks quite simple, but it carries a lot of power with it. With this simple viewset, we will have the power to query all pizzas in our database with a single request, as well as querying the resource by identifier.

Routers

We are getting rather close to a working solution for our REST framework. The final step we need to do is add the routing to the application itself. First, let's create a routes.py file in our pizza application, see Listing 4-7.

Listing 4-7. Pizza router

```
from rest_framework import routers

from pizza.viewswets import PizzaViewSet

router = routers.DefaultRouter()
router.register(r'api/v1/pizzas', PizzaViewSet)
```

Routers are the tool to map your RESTful resources to a standardized set of URLs, in the meantime simplifying the definitions of them.Here we are only using the default router, however, you can utilize various routers that give you different capabilities, such as automatic prefixing.

Now that we have added our router, we will simply link it to the urls.py file in the tizza module as described in Listing 4-8.

Listing 4-8. Pizza URL configs added

```
from pizza.routers import router

...

urlpatterns = [
    ....
    url(r'^', include(router.urls)),
    url(r'^api-auth/', include('rest_framework.urls',
    namespace='rest_framework'))
]
```

It's time to try out our new functionalities. First, let's try to get the pizza with the first id.

```
curl -X GET http://localhost:8000/api/v1/pizzas/1/
{"id":1,"title":"Quattro formaggi","description":"Cheesy"}
```

There we go. Now let's try without the id of the pizza.

```
curl -X GET http://localhost:8000/api/v1/pizzas/
[{"id":1,"title":"Quattro formaggi","description":"Cheesy"},
{"id":2,"title":"Diavolo","description":"Spicy!"}]
```

As you can see, the API has automatically returned all the pizza in the database. This is a very convenient feature that required 0 extra logic on our end. Let's try a pizza that doesn't exist in our database.

```
curl -i -X GET http://localhost:8000/api/v1/pizzas/42/
HTTP/1.1 404 Not Found
Date: Wed, 03 Jul 2019 18:00:29 GMT
Server: WSGIServer/0.2 CPython/3.6.5
Content-Type: application/json
Vary: Accept, Cookie
Allow: GET, PUT, PATCH, DELETE, HEAD, OPTIONS
X-Frame-Options: SAMEORIGIN
Content-Length: 23
```

```
{"detail":"Not found."}
```

There. Django REST Framework has automatically given us a 404 response without even writing an extra line of code on our end. This way it becomes very easy to write backend services that are there to host data for other systems.

This is already pretty mind blowing, however, it's not everything. Let's navigate to our browser and check out `http://localhost:8000/api/v1/ pizzas/`. You can see a representation of this page in Figure 4-1.

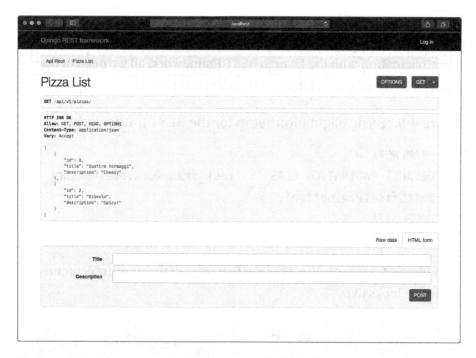

Figure 4-1. *The admin interface provided by the Django REST Framework*

We've also received a complete user interface where we can work with the resources. This functionality can be very useful when there are multiple teams maintaining multiple services with resources everywhere. This user interface gives the consumers of the API a way to interact with the resources without reading an extensive amount of documentation.

Some of you who are more familiar with web services and REST might be familiar with the concept of pagination. A couple of requests ago, we've queried all pizzas from the service, which is a useful feature, however, it will cause a huge issue after our users have created hundreds, or even thousands of resources that we'd return to the clients every time they require information. This can be exceptionally painful when people are using their mobile devices with only cellular data. This is one of the reasons why the concept of pagination came up. Essentially, the idea is that the client gives an offset and a batch size and receives resources that

85

are somehow indexed from offset to offset + batch size. The concept is quite simple, although often requires implementation on the client side. To enable pagination with the Django REST Framework, all we need to do is add the following lines in Listing 4-9 to our **settings.py** file.

Listing 4-9. Basic pagination setup for the REST framework

```
REST_FRAMEWORK = {
    'DEFAULT_PAGINATION_CLASS': 'rest_framework.pagination.
    LimitOffsetPagination',
    'PAGE_SIZE': 5
}
```

In Figure 4-2 you can see how the first page of the now implemented pagination looks like:

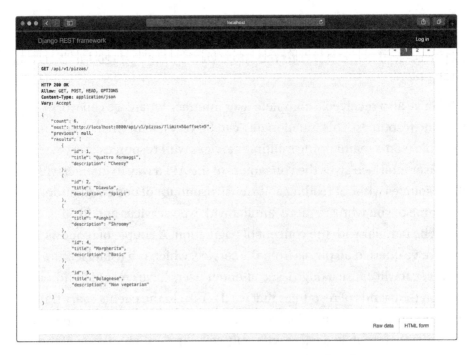

Figure 4-2. *The list of the first five pizzas in the database*

As you can see, we have 6 pizzas in total in our database, the endpoint returned us 5 of those and gave us the URL of the next page that we can use afterwards. After querying that one, you can see in Figure 4-3 that we only receive 1 pizza on the second page.

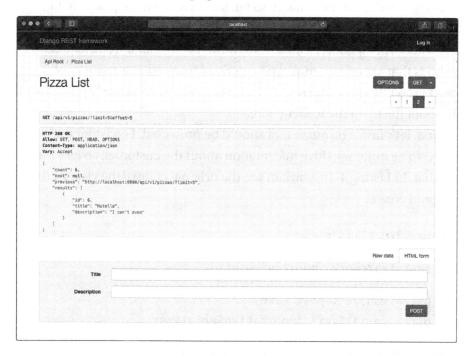

Figure 4-3. *The second page of the pagination*

EXERCISE 4-2: THE REST FRAMEWORK IN ACTION

We've read a lot about the Django REST Framework now, time to put it in action. Using the framework, create RESTful APIs for all the resource types that we've created in chapter 2.

Serving the resources is great and all, however, if you don't protect the resources that your customers are working with, you might as well leave business immediately. Let's talk about authenticating and authorizing clients, to make sure that they only access the correct resources.

Authentication

We've talked a lot about protecting data in chapter 2 when we were learning about the basic permission systems that Django offers. We've kind of ignored this functionality so far, however, with the power of the REST framework, we can easily implement authentication features that will protect our customer's data. If we went through all the authentication methods that are offered and can be derived from the framework, we would probably spend the rest of the book here. So we are only going to talk about the tip of the iceberg here.

First, let's find a resource that should be protected. I consider the "Likes" to be quite sensitive information about the customer, so let's roll with that. In Listing 4-10, you can see the original code of the viewset that we would create:

Listing 4-10. Like viewset

```
from rest_framework import viewsets

from pizza.models import Like
from pizza.serializers import LikeSerializer

class LikeViewSet(viewsets.ModelViewSet):
    queryset = Like.objects.all()
    serializer_class = LikeSerializer
```

The first question that we usually need to ask ourselves, is who should be able to access this resource? First off, we can say that if someone has a certain master password, they can access all the likes. For this, we can utilize the power of the bearer token authorization.

The bearer token authorization is basically nothing else but having a password that is stored somewhere on the resource owner's machine and clients who have access to this password can access resources on the server as well. You might recall from the previous chapter where we said that credentials of 12 factor apps should be stored in the environment. Although, the REST framework does have a built in token based authentication, it only supports tokens that are stored in the database of the application. Since this goes against the principles that we've learned in chapter 2, when we were talking about configurations coming from the environment, we are going to move forward and create an authentication class ourselves. Keep in mind, that this is not going against principles here, but it's 100% supported and recommended by Django REST Framework, see the solution in Listing 4-11.

Listing 4-11. Bearer token authorization for the REST framework

```python
import base64

from rest_framework import authentication, exceptions

from tizza.settings import CLIENT_TOKENS

class BearerTokenAuthentication(authentication.
BaseAuthentication):

    def authenticate(self, request):
        try:
            authorization_header = request.META['HTTP_
            AUTHORIZATION']
            _, token_base64 = authorization_header.split(' ')
            token = base64.b64decode(token_base64.encode())
            client, password = token.split(':')
            if CLIENT_TOKENS[client] == password:
                return None, None
            else:
                raise exceptions.AuthenticationFailed("Invalid
                authentication token")
```

```
    except KeyError:
        raise exceptions.AuthenticationFailed("Missing
        authentication header")
    except IndexError:|
        raise exceptions.AuthenticationFailed("Invalid
        authentication header")
```

Let's quickly go through the code so we are all on the same page. The first thing that might look weird is that we are loading this constant called CLIENT_TOKENS from the settings of the application. This should be a dictionary that is populated with the os module with all the enabled client identifiers and their respective tokens in it. Here's an example:

```
CLIENT_TOKENS = {
    'pizza-service': 'super-secret-password-for-the-pizza-
    service',
    'other-service': 'another-secret-password',
}
```

The way we can implement a custom authentication method is by overriding the BaseAuthentication class provided by the framework. All we need to do is implement the authenticate method that receives the request itself. Here, we fetch the Authorization header and then parse it's contents using the base64 module. The string that we expect here looks like: pizza-service:super-secret-password-for-the-pizza-service, which we will split by the colon and get the name of the client application and the password that they are using to access the resource. If we find the hashed password in our settings for the given client, we are good to go. Normally, you'd return a User object as the first value returned in the tuple, but it's not all that important in our case, since we give full access on authentication.

To try it out you will need to encode the passwords in base 64 and do a request that looks like this:

```
curl -X GET -H "Authorization: Bearer
cGl6emEtc2VydmljZTpzdXBlci1zZWNyZXQtcGFzc3dvcmQtZm9yLXRoZS1wa
Xp6YS1zZXJ2aWNlCg==
" http://localhost:8000/api/v1/pizzas/6/
{"id":6,"title":"Nutella","description":"I can't even"}
```

You can see that the response works just like before. Nothing special here. However, let's try it out without the header.

```
curl -X GET http://localhost:8000/api/v1/pizzas/6/
{"detail":"Missing authentication header"}
```

Also, we can try with an invalid token:

```
curl -X GET -H "Authorization: Bearer ijustwantin=" http://
localhost:8000/api/v1/pizzas/6/
{"detail":"Invalid authentication header"}
```

So, where did we get? We've been able to create a basic authentication method for our services that we can reuse in the future in various other ones. We can use the bearer token based authentication between service to service communication in the future. The way you generate and distribute these tokens is completely up to you. In an ideal world the tokens are dynamic and can be rotated often and on-demand.

This is all fine and dandy, however, in an ideal world we have multiple types of authentication. We don't want all users to have full access to all objects after all, right? Now, the REST framework has a type of authentication that is called SessionAuthentication. Sessions are a basic way of how Django handles the recognition of logged in users, sessions are set when a user logs in to the system and are disabled when the session expires, or the user logs out deliberately. Let's do a quick overview of how you can configure sessions in Django:

Database - In this version, you'd use the database as the session backend. Every time a session is set, there will be a database call made. In this case, the session information is still coming from the client side, however, it usually represents the ID of the session in the form of a cookie. To use this, you will need to enable **django.contrib.sessions** in your installed apps list and run a **manage.py** migrate to create the session database tables. This is generally considered the most basic form of sessions. It is quite easy to maintain until a certain scale, after that your database might get overwhelmed easily.

Cache - Caches are a great way to store sessions. Similar to the database approach, this might crunch under higher load, also, it might be less fault tolerant, since, for all cache restarts, all logged in users will be logged out. Can be used in conjunction with the database based backed. To use, you will need to assign **django.contrib.sessions.backends.cache** to your **SESSION_ENGINE** variable in **settings.py**.

Cookies - Cookies are also an excellent way to store sessions. Cookies can hold signed data with each request the user does to your platform. With the signed data, you can store information about their session, their authentication information and such. Session cookies are signed with a **SECRET_KEY** set in the **settings.py** of your Django application. Session cookies are inexpensive in space on the server, however, they can be expensive on the network communication that affects your users, so keep that in mind. To use, set **django.contrib.sessions.backends. signed_cookies** as the value of **SESSION_ENGINE**.

After learning about the 12 factors and the session methodologies that we've taken a look here, you might have gotten the impression that one of the best solutions for sessions in a distributed system might be cookies, and you're not wrong. The distributed nature of cookies, the fact that you can set expiration on them and the fact that you can set them up not to be accessible programmatically through the browser gives them a top spot on this list. The following exercises 4-3 and 4-4 will focus on extending our knowledge about authentication and cookies.

EXERCISE 4-3: AUTHENTICATION

Now that we've learned about it, try out the cookie based authentication, do some exploration with it. Set the values that are required and log in through the login page that we've built in the previous chapters. Check the cookies, their expiration, and if you can understand their contents.

EXERCISE 4-4: EXTENDED SESSIONS

We've already learned a lot about sessions and the session cookie, however, there's still a lot to explore. In this exercise I urge you to create a new authentication backend that gets a custom cookie called pizza-auth and loads it into the request auth. The pizza-auth cookie should be encrypted and should be assigned to the response of the login request of the user.

We've talked a lot about the synchronous world. As you can see, REST and synchronous communication has a lot of benefits, however, if you have too many services calling too many others, it is very easy to make your system sluggish. One solution that the industry came up with to solve this issue is asynchronous communication and queueing systems.

Asynchronous Communication

Synchronicity between systems offers clear communication and a simple way to reason about the application. Whenever you ask for an operation, the request is processed, done and then when you receive a response, you can be sure that what you wanted was either successful or failed, but it has been done nevertheless. However, sometimes if we stick to synchronous communication only, we can run into various difficulties in the application design. Consider the following example:

We are progressing well with the tizza application, people are using it and the architecture is evolving well as well, with multiple microservices in place now owned and developed by multiple teams. It's the year 2018 a sunny day in February and our head of security informs us that GDPR is coming up soon. For us to be GDPR compatible, we need to ensure that all user uploaded information, including likes and attended events, needs to be removed. Now, the team sat down to brainstorm about the issue at hand, and came up with the architecture plan in Figure 4-4.

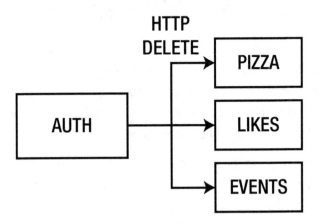

Figure 4-4. *Simple solution for GDPR*

As you can see, the solution is quite straightforward: upon user deletion from the auth database, there is a remote call to each service that holds the virtual value of the user. As a first version, this might be a good idea, however, there are various issues that this brings:

1. How will it scale? - So, now that this is done, every time we introduce a new service that holds a "pointer" to user objects needs to be added to this list? What is the point when we have way too many requests here and user deletion becomes unbearable?

2. Who owns the code? - What happens if the second remote call fails? Should the people who own the user information keep this code maintained and reliable, or every team owns their own small piece of code in this logic? Who will wake up in the middle of the night if this code needs some massage?

3. Who depends on who? - So far, the other services were depending on the user information being present in the auth service. However, now the auth service also depends on the other applications, making the system more coupled than it's supposed to be.

As you can see, we have plenty of issues with this approach. Luckily, there are solutions to reduce the coupling and make ownership cleaner in the system. We call these systems queues.

Concept of the Queue

You might remember learning about queues in high school or university. Now, imagine the same concept, just on the architectural level. An application in your system publishes messages to a broker or topic, which then later puts the messages on a queue, which will be consumed by workers. Figure 4-5 provides a simple overview of how the above example would work.

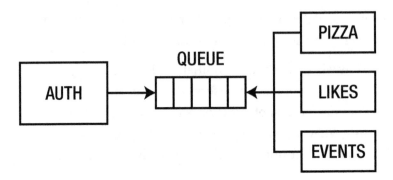

Figure 4-5. *Concept of a queue for GDPR*

As you can see, the auth service publishes a message that a user has been removed from the system. The message is published to a broker that pushes the message to three separate queues. One that removes the likes, one that removes the attendance and one that removes the uploaded pizzas.

What are the benefits of this?

1. We've scaled - Now we don't need to create a new call for each deletion that we need to handle, we can just create a new queue and bind it to the broker. This way, we stay fast on the calling side.

2. We've cleaned up ownership - You need to delete customer information? Just listen to this message, implement a handler for it and you're good to go. Removing the user information is in each individual team's ownership now, meaning that the team who are owning the auth service don't need to know about each individual service that stores information about users.

3. Dependencies are loosened - The system became less coupled by removing the hard dependencies between the various services. There's still some

coupling, but at least the publishing side doesn't
need to know about it. Let's say that events will
be handled by a third party from tomorrow and
we will not need to care of GDPR there, if we have
the queueing system in place, all we need to do is
remove the processor that was connected to the
events application and we are done, the auth team
does not need to worry about anything. However,
in the former solution, we would need to create a
change request for the auth team.

Unfortunately, Django does not have a super convenient support of
writing consumers for these queues. So for this part of the book, we are
going to leave the Djangoverse for a couple of paragraphs and look into
framework agnostic solutions in Python for the asynchronous problem.

Example Solution - RabbitMQ

The first tool that we are going to take a look at is RabbitMQ. RabbitMQ
has been built over the advanced message queueing protocol in the
mid 2000s. It is one of the most popular tools that are being used today
for asynchronous communication in large systems. Companies like
Reddit, 9GAG, HelloFresh and even stock exchanges use the powers of
this excellent tool to produce and consume millions of messages each
day in they systems. If you would like to learn more about alternatives,
I recommend taking a look at Amazon SQS or Apache Kafka. For the
purpose of Python tools, we are going to use the **pika** package that was
created for RabbitMQ.

pip install pika

Let's take a look at the core concepts of how it works.

Producer

Producers are part of RabbitMQ that are going to assemble and publish the messages we would like to have consumed asynchronously. In most cases, this code will live in your Django services. Let's continue with the user deletion and GDPR problem that we introduced previously. In our user viewset, we shall publish a message about our user being deleted through the API.

To get started, in Listing 4-12, we are going to create a small helper class so we can do producing in a simple way.

Listing 4-12. Basic publisher for RabbitMQ

```python
# pizza/utils/producer.py
import json
import pika
import sys

from django.conf import settings

class Producer:
    def __init__(self, host, username, password)
        self.connection = pika.BlockingConnection(
            pika.URLParameters(f'amqp://{username}:{password}@
            {host}:5672')
        )
        self.channel = connection.channel()
        self.exchanges = []

    def produce(exchange, body, routing_key="):
        if exchange not in self.exchanges:
            channel.declare_exchange(exchange=exchange)
            self.exchanges.append(exchange)
```

```
    self.channel.basic_publish(
        exchange=exchange,
        routing_key=routing_key,
        body=json.dumps(body)
    )

producer = Producer(
    host=os.environ.get('RABBITMQ_HOST'),
    username=os.environ.get('RABBITMQ_USERNAME'),
    password=os.environ.get('RABBITMQ_PASSWORD'),
)
```

A couple of things to explain here:

- We've used Python's global object pattern, which is quite common in the Python world when you'd like to create objects that behave like singletons. The way we are going to use the publisher is just from **pizza.utils. producer import producer**.

- When we are creating a connection, we are using the AMQP DSN. This is actually recommended by the AMQP documentation. Make sure to create separate users and passwords for all your applications that will connect to the RabbitMQ broker.

- A couple of terminologies that came up:

    - **Exchange**: An exchange you can think of as a logical separator of your message types. For example, you might want to publish messages about users to the users exchange or messages about likes to the likes exchange. Aside from being a domain separator, exchanges also decide how many queues should receive the message Many companies don't

use exchanges and that's completely fine.
Exchanges need to be created manually (as
you can see).

- **Routing key**: Routing keys we use so we can make
  sure that the right messages get to the right places.
  For example, we might have the likes system and
  the pizzas system sitting separately and listening to
  the user deleted messages. In this case, we would
  create two routing keys, **likes.delete** and **pizzas.
  delete** on the **users** exchange.

- A tiny best practice has been hidden in the publishing
  of the message, which is sending a JSON body. Later in
  this chapter we are going to talk about why structuring
  your messages is very important (just like in REST).

We can use the above code as shown in Listing 4-13:

Listing 4-13. Using the basic publisher to publish user deleted
information

```
from pizza.utils.producer import producer

...

class UsersViewSet(viewsets.ModelViewSet):
    queryset = User.objects.all()
    serializer_class = UserSerializer

    def destroy(self, request, *args, **kwargs):
        user = self.get_object()
        response = super().destroy(request, *args, **kwargs)
        producer.produce(
```

```
        exchange='user',
        body={'user_id': user.id},
        routing_key='user.deleted'
    )
    return response
```

Now whenever a user object gets deleted through our APIs, we will send out a message to the users exchange that a user got deleted.

Consumers

Now, systems that are interested in this message can create a queue and bind it to the exchange with the given routing key. Here's an implementation for a simple consumer in Listing 4-14:

Listing 4-14. Basic consumer implementation

```
import os
import pika

class Consumer:
    def __init__(self, host, username, password):
        self.host = host
        self.username = username
        self.password = password

    def _init_channel(self):
        connection = pika.BlockingConnection(
            pika.URLParameters(f'amqp://{self.username}:{self.
            password}@{self.host}:5672')
        )
        return connection.channel()

    def _init_queue(exchange, queue_name, routing_key):
        queue = channel.queue_delcare(queue=queue_name)
```

```
        channel.queue_bind(exchange=exchange queue=queue_name,
        routing_key=routing_key)
        return result.method.queue

    def consume(self, exchange, queue_name, routing_key,
    callback):
        channel = self._init_channel()
        queue_name = self._init_queue()
        channel.basic_consume(
            queue=queue_name,
            on_message_callback=callback,
        )

consumer = Consumer(
    host=os.environ.get('RABBITMQ_HOST'),
    username=os.environ.get('RABBITMQ_USERNAME'),
    password=os.environ.get('RABBITMQ_PASSWORD'),
)
```

Now, when we want to use this consumer, we just need to write a simple Python script that we can store next to the backend application code itself. We can actually write a Django script to extend our application and use all the benefits that we would have when we are running the Django application or the shell as shown in Listing 4-15.

Listing 4-15. Basic consumer usage

```
import json

from django.core.management.base import BaseCommand,
CommandError

from pizza.models import Likes
from pizza.utils.consumer import consumer
```

```python
class ConsumeUserDeleted(BaseCommand):
    help = "Consumes user deleted messages from RabbitMQ"

    def _callback(channel, method, properties, body):
        payload = json.loads(body)
        user_id = payload.get('user_id')
        if user_id is not None:
            likes = Likes.objects.filter(user_id=user_id)
            likes.delete()

    def handle(self, *args, **options):
        consumer.consume(
            exchange='users',
            queue='users-deleted',
            routing_key='user.deleted',
            callback=self._callback,
        )
```

Now we've created a simple distributed messaging system. It is interesting to know that consumers and producers can live in different machines and even different cloud providers. You can set up a system on your own machine to consume messages from an exchange for debugging purposes, for example.Try deleting users through your APIs and see how the rest of the system will elegantly handle the requests. In the next section, we are going to take a look at some of the best practices that might be worth following when you are introducing an asynchronous queueing system to your architecture.

Asynchronous Best Practices

All these things that we've looked at so far seem quite simple. However, when you start working at scale, it might get a little messy. We are going to go through a couple of best practices that you should take into account when building these asynchronous components.

Message Payloads

One of the most difficult things to do is making sure that when the message producer changes the message payload, the consumers don't get confused and run into exceptions. For this, it might be a good idea to version your payloads, just like we've been versioning the REST APIs.

There are multiple ways to version your payloads. The most common way of doing this is to add the version of the message into the routing key. Some forums recommend using semantic versioning for the message versions which makes the routing key look something like this:

user.deleted.1.2.3

To decompose:

- user.deleted - The original routing key

- 1. The major version of the message. This number should increase when there's a breaking change in the published message. For example: the user id becomes a string instead of a number.

- 2. Minor version. Some new feature has entered the message, it should not break the message consuming. For example, the message starts containing the email address of the deleted user as well. Some systems might need this information to complete their operations, but it doesn't affect old systems.

- 3. Patch version. No major changes and no new features have changed in the message, could indicate bugfixes in the message payload.

Now, if you like to keep things simple, you can just keep 1 number, the major number from the above list. In that case, there will be a little bit less work involved.

Let's do a short exercise where there are two teams: the auth team and the likes team. The auth team has decided to change user identifiers from a number to a uuid for security reasons. This means that the messages need to be updated as well. So, what does the version migration look like in this case?

1. **auth** team sends out a notification that there will be a change in the user model in the identifiers at the beginning of their project to notify all teams.

2. **auth** team implements uuids and publishes the following messages at the same time:

   a. ```
publisher.publish(
        exchange='user',
        body={'user_id': user.id},
        routing_key='user.deleted.1.0.0')
```

   b. ```
publisher.publish(
        exchange='user',
        body={'user_uuid': user.uuid},
        routing_key='user.deleted.2.0.0')
```

3. **auth** team sends out a deprecation notification of their 1.0.0 message to the company and gives a reasonable deadline for the migration.

4. **likes** team plans and implements listening to the new version of the user deletion.

5. **auth** team removes the old version of the code.

Sounds idealistic, I know, however, this is the way you can ensure that there will be no outages during implementation of breaking features.

Handling Broker Outages

One of the issues with queueing systems are broker outages. Basically, when the central queueing component stops working, there could be a myriad of issues:

- Lost messages: Probably the worst one of them all. When messages are lost and there's no trace of them whatsoever, the overall state of your application gets skewed. This doesn't only cause issues at the given moment, but it might cause discrepancies in the future as well. Just imagine a payment state machine that gets confused about the customer's current status.

- Disconnected producers and consumers: During a broker outage, the network might give up as well, having producers and consumers - often silently - disconnect from the broker itself. If these systems are forgotten to be reconnected, it might cause an unpleasant surprise in the future.

One of the first things you need to do to avoid catastrophes like this, is to have proper monitoring and alerting systems over your broker cluster. The earlier you know about an outage, the faster you can react to it. If you have the resources, an even better solution could be to outsource hosting your broker to professionals. If it's not your core competency, you should probably not try to engineer it.

Another solution that you can do on-premise is to use various design patterns to improve resiliency of you cluster. The most important thing that you need to protect is data integrity and for this, there's a pattern called outbox.

Some of you might be familiar with the outbox pattern, for those who are not, here's a refresher: the outbox is a software engineering pattern, primarily used in applications which send out synchronous or asynchronous messages, where all the messages get stored in a storage and then get dispatched by an external process from that given storage. The dispatcher is oftentimes called the outbox worker. Figure 4-6 a quick overview of the architecture.

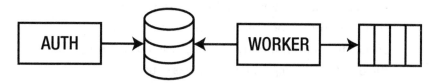

Figure 4-6. *The outbox architecture*

As you can see, the service wants to publish a message to the RabbitMQ broker. First, it stores the message in a database and then the outbox worker process picks up the message and publishes it to the broker. At first glance, this might seem like a waste of time, however, if you think about it, the messages only get removed from the cold storage, if publishing was absolutely successful. This means that if the broker is down, messages are still kept intact.

As you can see, asynchronous communication is an incredibly powerful tool for maximizing speed, efficiency and decoupling your systems even further. There are a couple of things, I'd like to mention about the drawbacks of asynchronous communication before we move on to the next chapter.

- Data duplication: I think I mentioned this one already somewhere. I would like to emphasize it again. With asynchronous systems, it becomes very tempting to duplicate data across your cluster, since you gotta stay fast, right? Well, once you start duplicating data, you will get into an endless spiral of making sure that everything on your side is correct. First you will just listen to user created events, then address updated, and then one day you will forget to listen to email updated in one of your applications and data will begin to be inconsistent across your cluster. You don't want that sort of headache, trust me. My advice is to keep data duplication to a minimum.

- Asynchronous breeds asynchronous: As you've seen with the outbox pattern, we've created an asynchronous solution (periodically fetching from the database) to a problem that was caused by asynchronous communication in the first place. This seems to be a common phenomenon in asynchronous systems. In general, asynchronous systems are harder to test, and they are more difficult to reason about. If we add more async over it, we are not going to make it any easier for ourselves.

- Race conditions: Now, race conditions can exist in both synchronous and asynchronous systems, however, in my experience, they are way more manageable in synchronous systems. The biggest issues arise when you're mixing the two without much thought. Imagine the following situation:

  - Service A publishes message M that service B and C listen to

  - Service C requires some data from service B for the message processing that depends on service B having processed the message

  - If service B is not fast enough, we have lost information in service C

  If your team decides to go with a solution for a problem that represents the above description, I'd

recommend building a strong requeueing logic for
the service that is the most dependent on the data,
in this case C. If C can handle errors from the other
services, you're good to go. However, in real life, the
complexity of race conditions can be much higher
than the one explained here. I also recommend
always monitoring the connections, messages that
have not been acknowledged, exceptions and the
queue throughputs to make sure that data is not
being lost.

Conclusion

We've covered a lot about communication between various services
in our systems. All communication types have their advantages and
disadvantages. Every situation will require you to rethink what tools you
are going to use for the given problem. Nailing the communication layer
is perhaps the biggest challenge when building microservices. With these
tools at your hand, you will definitely not make huge mistakes.

## CHAPTER 5

From Monolith to Microservice

Now that we've learned what are the qualities that we are aiming for in a service and how we can connect them to each other, it is time for us to take a closer look at actual techniques, which will help us to migrate from our monolithic application to a microservice architecture. Please take note that the techniques described here are not silver bullets and you will definitely need to modify them for your own use-case, however, experience shows that these general methodologies give an excellent starting point for a successful migration. Keep in mind, some of the steps described in this chapter are parallelizable, so if you have more people to help you, so can speed things up a little.

Before you Start

By the time you've reached so far in the book, you probably understand that migrating your monolithic system to microservices is not going to be just a walk in the park. There will be serious human and financial costs of delivery. Even estimating delivery to your stakeholders might be a huge difficulty (at least in the beginning), so let's run through the basic costs that you will need to calculate with.

© Akos Hochrein 2019
A. Hochrein, *Designing Microservices with Django*,
https://doi.org/10.1007/978-1-4842-5358-8_5

Human Costs

Naturally, we are mostly talking about the costs of refactoring your codebase. In the early stages of the project, you will require much more effort than when you've migrated multiple components. Be very conservative with your estimations in the beginning and get a bit more strict with yourself and your team after you have the tooling in place that we will be talking here in chapter 5 and later in chapter 6.

To my experience, there are two areas where the migration could be very difficult and could significantly increase the coding costs of your migration:

1. Operations-related - How to deploy and how to scale your new services can always be a critical and dividing question when moving to a new type of architecture. Deployment of your monolith might have been a person running a couple of scripts to rsync data to a remote server and then restarting the application, monitoring (which is a very important aspect when you're changing your infrastructure in such a big way) might be rowing in the same boat. When you move to microservices, this might not cut it in the long run. At minimum, you will need to collect these executables and organize them in a usable way so that others in the company have access to it as well. We will cover more operations related topics in the next chapter.

2. Code-related - You know when code is messy like a bowl of spaghetti and not neatly organized as a well sliced pizza? Keeping your codebase clean in a high velocity environment where there's constant push

for delivery can be a huge challenge. Unkempt code
can be one of the other big costs when you would
like to migrate.

Depending on the size of your company and monolithic application,
it is a good idea to have a dedicated team that takes care of tooling,
documentation, guidelines and best practices for the other teams that have
the domain knowledge for the migration of their components. If you're
operating with hundreds of engineers with a monolith of millions of lines
of code, this is practically a must have. If your scale is somewhat smaller, it
could be a convenience.

Some companies like to implement emergency or "tiger" teams
when a critical component needs to be migrated due to resiliency or
other concerns. This could be a good way of moving a lot of software into
different systems, however, it is highly recommended to pay attention
to the handover of the code and implement intense knowledge sharing
sessions between the migration and the maintenance teams.

Now let's see the sort of hardware and infrastructure costs that we will
need to implement.

Infrastructure Costs

Moving to microservices can have another expensive implication, which
is the cost of having enough machines to run the new system (and, for a
while, the old system as well). What does this mean exactly? Let's consider
the following scenario:

Our tizza application that runs on two 10 core machine with 128
gigabytes of RAM powering them. During the migration planning, we've
identified 6 systems that we can logically shard our application into. Now,
let's do the math:

Depending on the load on the systems we will need either single core or dual core machines for the new services. Probably the system that handles authentication and likes will require 2 cores and 8 gigabytes of ram, whereas the pizza metadata storage might just take a single core and 4 gigabytes of RAM. We can average the number of CPUs for the entire cluster to 8 and the total memory costs to 32 gigabytes. Since, we used to work with 2 machines for the monolith, we should also raise the numbers here, we don't want to decrease resiliency after all.

As you try to scale down your systems into smaller but more efficient pieces, it is a very human reaction to underscale your cluster and underestimate the amount of raw power that is required to run your software safely. A general rule of thumb that I like to follow when creating new microservies, is to run 3 copies of the service on different (virtual or physical) machines for high availability.

For confident people, the above statement can be eliminated with a great cloud provider, super lightweight applications and a well configured autoscaling system.

Note   Autoscaling is when you define rules about the number of servers you would like to run in your cluster. The rule can be a function of memory or CPU usage, number of live connections to your cluster, time of day, or other values that your cloud provider might allow you to use.

As you can see, we've raised the total number of cores in the system from 20 to 24 and the memory has remained at about 128 gigabytes, with a grand total of 96. You will quickly notice that these numbers tend to grow quicker than expected in a real life environment and depending on your provider, it might cause devastating costs to your business.

My advice is to overshoot in the beginning for safety and revisit your application every now and then to make sure that the hardware is not an overkill for the software.

I Made the Call, What's Next?

Probably the biggest question that has come up in your head while reading this book so far is how to convince your company that this is a worthwhile investment for them and not just a fun refactoring for you. Well, this is an age-long debate that has no silver bullet to it. I will try to give your a couple of pointers so you can get started:

- Technical debt as a first-class project citizen: Oftentimes people think that these sorts of changes will require big projects where multiple people to collaborate at a grandiose scale. As you will see from this chapter, it's not the case. The first advice I can give is to move technical debt and refactoring into feature projects that you'd need to deliver to the company. Make sure that you're transparent and reasonable about this so you can do it in the future as well. Also, if you receive a no, that's fine as well, just be persistent about it, it's all about the conversation. Putting technical debt related tasks into feature projects enables engineers to be more efficient with both areas. There are less context switches, making both the feature development and the technical debt work more efficient. The engineers will also be happier, since they will leave higher quality work behind themselves.

- Measure your results: If you were able to squeeze in some refactoring here and there, show your colleagues how much easier it is to use your new database interface or how much faster it is to deliver a new feature with the functions that you've extracted and make sure to tell your product owner or manager as well. If you have metrics to prove that your work has been worth it, it's even better. These metrics are often hard to find and come up with, some of them could be related to application speed, some of them related to delivery speed (i.e. how fast does a new feature get shipped because we made this and this technical change in the service), or even the number of bug tickets that get addressed to your team.

- Be candid: Make sure that you measure and explain the costs to all stakeholders and you do it honestly. This will be a big project, no point in making it look small. People do need to understand that feature development will slow down for a while and the processes around it will be different in the future.

- Sometimes no is fine: It's completely possible that your company is just not ready for a grand scale migration like this. In this case, make sure that you and your company are as successful as possible, so you can have resiliency problems in the near future. In the introductory chapter, we've seen the catastrophe scenarios for a streaming application. A shock like this can cause a company to change their mindset, you will, however, need to reach that scale first with the business. If you receive too many "no"s, then it's probably time to rethink your own scope and reduce it to the smallest that you can do, to show the company how the process would look like and what the value of it is.

As you can see, making a call like this can be very difficult for a company in many ways. The best strategy is oftentimes to be patient, leave your frustrations behind and employ refactoring techniques and tools that you've acquired through this book, they will come in handy in the future.

Now that we are done with understanding the costs of the errand, it's time to start migration our application, first, by preparing the data.

Data Preparation

Before we get into the juicy parts of refactoring our application, we need to make sure that the data we would like to transfer is, well, transferable, meaning that it is easy to copy it from one place to another and is not coupled too much with other data domains in our system. In addition to this, we need to find the clusters of data that seem to live together from a domain and business perspective.

Domain Sharding

As you can see, we can identify the following chunks of data that live together:

- User related information

- Pizza and restaurant information

- Likes and match groups

- Events and event related integrations

The domain dictates the above, however, there's still a lot of hard coupling between certain parts of the above. Let's take a look at the pizzeria model:

```
class Pizzeria(models.Model):
    owner = models.ForeignKey(UserProfile, on_delete=models.
    CASCADE)
    address = models.CharField(max_length=512)
    phone = models.CharField(max_length=40)
```

As you can see, we have a hard foreign key rule on the owner field with the user profile model. The first thing that you will need to do is make sure that these foreign keys will be pointing to virtual objects, where the foreign object can be thought of as a reference as such:

```
class Pizzeria(models.Model):
    owner_user_profile_id = models.PositiveIntegerField()
    address = models.CharField(max_length=512)
    phone = models.CharField(max_length=40)
```

Why is this beneficial? Well, now the objects are less coupled and more trust-based. Pizzas will trust the system that there's a user with a given user profile id and can live in their own separate environment. There are no hard coded database rules that will bind pizzas and user profiles together anymore, which is very liberating, but also very scary at the same time.

What do we lose with this?

- Cascading deletes are gone. You will need to manually delete linked objects.

- Some convenience methods provided by the Django ORM, such as select_related, are not available anymore.

Naturally, you can (and should) keep coupling between models that reside in the same database, so you retain the convenience methods and with it some speed and reliability for your queries.

If you're not a database wizard, this can seem like a difficult errand to run. However, you might remember a powerful tool that we've learned about in chapter 2 called migrations. You can very easily create a new migration which will replace foreign keys with identifiers. Listing 5-1 provides an example for the pizzeria.

Listing 5-1. Example migration from model to id

```
def set_defaults(apps, schema_editor):
    Pizzeria = apps.get_model('pizza', 'pizzeria')
    for pizzeria in Pizzeria.objects.all().iterator():
        pizzeria.owner_user_profile_id = pizzeria.owner.id
        pizzeria.save()

def reverse(apps, schema_editor):
    pass

class Migration(migrations.Migration):

    dependencies = [
        ('pizza', '0002_pizzeria'),
    ]

    operations = [
        migrations.AddField(
            model_name='pizzeria',
            name='owner_user_profile_id',
            field=models.PositiveIntegerField(null=True),
            preserve_default=False,
        ),
        migrations.RunPython(set_defaults, reverse),
        migrations.AlterField(
            model_name='pizzeria',
            name='owner_user_profile_id',
```

```
            field=models.PositiveIntegerField(),
    ),
    migrations.RemoveField(
        model_name='pizzeria',
        name='owner',
    ),
]
```

Let's take a closer look at this code. After we've changed the model and ran the **makemigrations** command we've been prompted to give a default value for the new field that we've created, here we can give 0, it won't matter too much. To make sure that all the values are set right, we are going to alter the migration code the above way. The logic is the following:

1. We add a new field called **owner_user_profile_id** to the table. We set it as nullable, so the migrations can create it with no issues whatsoever.

2. We run a set of Python code that will set up the values for us accordingly:

    a. The **set_defaults** function fetches all values from the already created pizzerias and adds them to the new field. Just what we need.

    b. If we really need to, we can specify a reverse for this function. It will not be needed for now.

3. We alter the **owner_user_profile_id** field to be non-nullable.

4. We drop the **owner** field for good.

You can use the above template to almost all migration files. For tables with a high number of rows (i.e. it would be dangerous to load the entire database into memory), it is highly recommended to change the query in the set_defaults function to a bulk operation. Alternatively, for really big tables (we are talking about millions of business critical rows here), you might want to involve a database expert to aid with the migration.

You might get the hunch that if you run this migration, everything will crash. Well, this is completely true. The owner field on all pizzeria objects will be breaking code from there on in your codebase and this might cause some headache. Ideally, you would change all the code in your codebase to use the new field that was created to fetch the owner objects, however, there are some ways to protect us from breaking, for example with the use of Python properties, see Listing 5-2 below.

Listing 5-2. Using properties as model fields

```
class Pizzeria(models.Model):
    owner_user_profile_id = models.PositiveIntegerField()
    address = models.CharField(max_length=512)
    phone = models.CharField(max_length=40)

    @property
    def owner(self):
        return UserProfile.objects.get(id=self.owner_user_
        profile_id)
```

Using properties the above way can greatly speed up the migration process, however, it might cause issues in the long run, especially regarding performance, since we just moved from a very efficient database JOIN operation to another query that gets executed. However, you will later notice that this is not the biggest hit in speed that we will receive.Let's take a look at the next steps of the migration, where we will make sure that data will be accessible to both the old and the new systems.

Database Duplication

After you've decided which part of your application you would like to migrate and modified the database accordingly, it is time to set up a migration plan on the database level. I.e. it is time to prepare your new database that will host your models.

Probably the easiest way to get started with this is to set up replicas of your main database. The idea is that all writes will be copied to the replica, which will be used as read-only. Don't worry too much about setting up the replication for specific tables only, most of the time is only causes a headache and extra work. It's usually easier to just set up a full replication and just drop the tables from the new database that you won't need when the migration is ready.

Note   You can also set up master-master replication between the 2 databases, however, the technologies for this requires a lot of database expertise and give more room for error post-release.

Depending on the size and type of your database, the replication can take from minutes to days, so make sure to add this to your estimations when communicating to your line manager and team. To get started with this, you might want to take a look at how Amazon RDS does data replication. If you want to go a little bit deeper into the technology, there is great documentation on dev.mysql.com on how to setup replication for MySQL, and on the Postgres Wikipedia for Postgres.

Testing and Coverage

We've done some preparation. Now it's time to copy all the code... Just kidding. Ideally, this is the point where you make sure that your application will not break when you migrate code from one system to another.

To achieve this, the single most useful tool that you can use is testing. Django comes with it's own built in test framework with which you can test even the database level quite easily with it's included in-memory database, however, any unittest framework will do the job, such as **unittest2**, **pytest** or **nose**.

When it comes to how you can measure if you're doing well on the testing side, many teams and engineers recommend using tools like **coverage**, with which you can measure the number of lines of code you've tested in your application. However, this metric does not always measure the true value of your tests. The recommendation is that you cover the core business functionalities of your views and models. Ideally, if you're running backend application with some external communication methods exposed, you can also implement integration tests which would test the functionalities provided by your entire endpoint or consumer. If you have the people, then you can also implement acceptance tests, which are usually very high level tests where an automated robot is clicking through your website and checking if the base user flows are successful or not. These are usually quite fragile and expensive to maintain, however, they can be life-savers as the last line of defence before a critical bug goes into production. An excellent acceptance testing framework is cucumber, you can read more about it at cucumber.io.

Now that we have covered our code with tests, it's time to start working on some tools, so we can migrate the codebase from one place to another.

Moving the Service

So far we did some work on the models that we wanted to migrate and prepared a new database. It's time to start working towards actually migrating the code.

Remote Models

Before we could copy the parts of the codebase that we would like
to operate in the separate system, we need to make sure that the
dependencies between the two codebases are manageable. So far we've
learned that Django and Python are quite flexible tools to build services
and to maintain them, however, we also learned that there's a huge
dependency on the data in the form of models. Consider the code snippet
in Listing 5-3 which we would like to migrate to a separate service:

Listing 5-3. Problematic function to extract

```
from pizza.models import Like
from user.models import UserProfile

def get_fullname_and_like_count(user_profile_id):
    user_profile = UserProfile.objects.get(id=user_profile_id)
    full_name = user_profile.first_name + ' ' + user_profile.
last_name
    likes = Likes.objects.count()
    return full_name, likes
```

No matter which service we would like to extract the above code,
we will face a dilemma. There are cross references to the models in the
function which can be difficult to solve. If we want to avoid data duplication
and clean the domain clean, we need to make sure that likes and user
profiles don't reside in both separate services and databases. For this, we
can do a refactoring technique that we're going to call remote models.

Remote models are a concept I've come across multiple times in
my career and they are a real lifesaver. The idea is, that if your apis are
uniform, you can very easily replace your database model calls with
remote calls using a simple search and replace in your codebase (at least in
most cases). See Listing 5-4 for an example remote model implementation.

Note   The code we will be looking at might not fit your needs perfectly, but it's a good starting point and exercise to start thinking with remote models.

Listing 5-4. The basic remote model

```python
import requests
import urllib.parse

from settings import ENTITY_BASE_URL_MAP

class RemoteModel:

    def __init__(self, request, entity, version):
        self.request = request
        self.entity = entity
        self.version = version
        self.url = f'{ENTITY_BASE_URL_MAP.get(entity)}/api/
{version}/{entity}'

    def _headers(self, override_headers=None):
        base_headers = {'content-type': 'application/json'}
        override_headers = override_headers or {}
        return {
            **request.META,
            **base_headers,
            **override_headers,
        }

    def _cookies(self, override_cookies=None):
        override_cookies = override_cookies or {}
        return {
            **self.request.COOKIES,
            **override_cookies,
        }
```

```python
    def get(self, entity_id):
        return requests.get(
            f'{self.url}/{entity_id}',
            headers=self._headers(),
            cookies=self._cookies())

    def filter(self, **conditions):
        params = f'?{urllib.parse.urlencode(conditions)}'
        if conditions else "
        return requests.get(
            f'{self.url}/{params}',
            headers=self._headers(),
            cookies=self._cookies())

    def delete(self, entity_id):
        return requests.delete(
            f'{self.url}/{entity_id}',
            headers=self._headers(),
            cookies=self._cookies())

    def create(self, entity_id, entity_data):
        return requests.put(
            f'{self.url}/',
            data=json.dumps(entity_data),
            headers=self._headers(),
            cookies=self._cookies())

    def update(self, entity_id, entity_data):
        return requests.post(
            f'{self.url}/{entity_id}'
            data=json.dumps(entity_data),
            headers=self._headers(),
            cookies=self._cookies())
```

That's a lot of code. Let's take a closer look at it. The first thing that you might notice is that the **RemoteModel** class' interface exposes a mixture of Django models and standards that we've established during our exploration of the REST framework. The get, filter, delete, create, update methods expose a Django model like interface for the sake of simple refactoring and domain familiarity, however, the implementations themselves involve a lot of words that we've encountered when we were examining the REST paradigms.

The **ENTITY_BASE_URL_MAP** is a convenience map that you can create in your settings file to specify unique url bases for each entity that you're working with.

All of this is quite simple so far. So where's the trick? You might've noticed that the request object is a required parameter when you're creating an instance of the remote model. Why is this? Simply put, we are using the request object to propagate the headers that we've received in the request itself. This way, if you're using headers or cookies for authentication, everything will be propagated without any issues.

After this, the usage of these models should be fairly easy. You can subclass the RemoteModel to your specific needs for convenience, like we have done in Listing 5-5:

Listing 5-5. Simple remote pizza

```
class RemotePizza(RemoteModel):

    def __init__(self, request):
        super().__init__(request, 'pizza', 'v1')
```

And then, you can do the following in your view functions, as shown in Listing 5-6:

Listing 5-6. Examples of remote pizza usage

```
pizza = RemotePizza(request).get(1)
pizzas = RemotePizza(request).filter(title__startswith='Marg')
RemotePizza(request).delete(1)
```

Note   The filter function will require additional implementation on the server side, since the Django REST Framework does not support them by default.

Drawbacks of remote models:

- Remote models can be slow - Depending on the network, the implementation, the hardware and sometimes the alignment of the stars, remote models can be much-much slower than their database counterparts. This slowness can also escalate as you start "chaining" remote methods over your architecture, by calling systems that call other systems that call other systems, etc.

- It's more fragile - In general, remote models are much more fragile than regular ones. Connections to the database are much more robust and enduring than connections that you do over HTTP.

- Bulk operations and loops need to be reviewed thoroughly - Sometimes unideal code gets copied during the migration process and, lets say, a for loop that had a database call through models in it becomes a HTTP call through the remote models. Due to the first point, this can be devastating if we're querying a large number of models.

- There's no serialization - If you're using this
  simple model, you will definitely lose the power of
  serialization, meaning that you will only receive a
  dict back as a response and not necessarily a model
  or a lost of models that you'd be expecting. This is
  not an unsolvable problem, you can look into Python
  dataclasses and modules like **dacite**.

Another good topic that comes up during the implementation of
remote models is caching. Caching is quite a difficult problem to solve, so
I recommend you not to implement it in your first iteration. One easy and
big win, that I've noticed over the years is to implement a request-level
cache in your service. What this means, is that the result of each remote
call is stored in some way on the request and does not need to be fetched
again from the remote service. What this allows you, is to do multiple
remote model calls to the same resource from your service in a view
function, yet not actually use the network to get the resource. This can save
a lot of network traffic even in the beginning.

Let's take a look at exercise 5-1, 5-2 and 5-3 that will help us work with
remote models a bit more.

EXERCISE 5-1: REMOTE MODELS FOR SERVICE TO SERVICE

The above model solves the issue of header and cookie propagation well
enough so that we can access data from various points of the system using
authentication methods such as sessions or authentication headers that we've
looked at in the previous chapters. However, this could cause issues if we
would like to use different tokens when we would like to call services without
user authentication. In this exercise, you're encouraged to design an extension
to the RemoteModel with which we can assign override authentication tokens
properly. There's already some code in place above which you can use.

EXERCISE 5-2: REMOTE OR NOT REMOTE

Remote models seem like a very powerful tool already, but can we make them even more powerful? Try to extend the RemoteModel class to be able to handle database calls when the model is available in a local database. Doing this change can enable you to speed up migrations in the future.

EXERCISE 5-3: REQUEST LEVEL CACHE

We've mentioned request level caching before, now it is time to test our Python and Django knowledge and implement it. Each time a remote model action is called, make sure to store the response in a cache that is tied to the request itself. You can use various caching libraries, like cachetools for this.

Working on our tooling was a lot of fun, time for the code migration.

The Code Migration

Probably the least exciting part of the entire migration. You need to copy the codebase that you would like the other systems to own. You will need to create a new Django project for these applications, find the settings and the utilities and copy all of it. Here are a couple of tips that I like to follow when I am at this point of the migration:

- Keep it simple - At this point, no need to worry too much about code duplication between services (unless you already have some tooling in place for this). Just make sure that your application gets up and running as soon as possible. We are going to delete the code in the monolith anyway.

- Follow the domain - Just like with data sharding, domain is key here as well. Make sure that the module that you'd like to move out is as isolated from the system as possible. What you'd like to aim for, is just copying an app from one codebase to another as-is.

- Tests are key - Some microservices that you create are monsters in themselves. For example, you might have a payments service that has an internal state machine and multiple integrations to various payment providers, you've made the decision to extract the entire domain in one piece. Make sure that your tests are in place, running and eventually not breaking. Testing such massive systems by hand is nigh impossible. Tests can also aid your in your migration, if you've missed some code or functionality here and there.

- Accept that you will lose speed first - It's one thing that the migration takes a while, but applications usually become slower during the early stages of their lifecycle. This is caused by the above negatives that we've examined with remote models. What you will notice, is that on the long run the owner team will take good care of their application and implement various speed enhancing features as the most knowledgeable engineers in their domain.

Release

The code is copied, all the tests are passing, it's time for the release.

Strategies

The first deployment of a new microservice is always a little messy and involves a lot of conversation around strategies and methodologies beforehand. Just as in most places in this book, there's no silver bullet for the release process, however, there are a couple of methodologies you can choose from, depending on your preparation, tools and the willingness of your team to wake up early.

Read first, write later - This strategy means that the microservice will first only run in read-only mode, meaning that traffic on it will not modify the data owned by it. One of my favourite strategies, which allows you to use both the monolith and the new microservice to access data at the same time. If you've chosen to set up read replication to your new database, well, it should be quite safe to use the APIs from the new service the provide read functionalities, for example fetching pizza metadata. This way, you can make sure that your application is running in production and only start writing data in it when you're confident that your infrastructure can handle it.

Rolling deployment - Basically means that you will send a percentage of your total traffic to the new microservice and leave the rest on the monolith, slowly but surely letting all traffic to be handled by the new system. With modern load-balancers and service meshes, this can be easily set up. This is not an option if you have chosen to create a read replica, since the writes that would happen on the new microservice's database would not get registered in the monolith's database.

Full traffic change - Probably the easiest to achieve and the fastest to revert. When you're confident that your service works, you switch the traffic on a given url to the new service. The process should be simple and easily reversible, such as changing a configuration on a website or a file.

Note   Naturally, there are many other release strategies that we could be talking about here. The main idea is to have context around the options that you have regarding risk, difficulty and preparation time so you can make an educated decision on how you want to tackle this problem.

Now that we have an idea about what strategy we'd like to use to release our service, let's take a look at how we are going to react when things inevitably break.

Handling Outages

In my experience, there's always some expected downtime when a new microservice is released. The good news is that this downtime can be minimal if you do a couple of small preparation steps beforehand:

- Create a playbook for reverting - Probably the most important thing you can do. Make sure that you have a step by step guide for the engineers to revert the traffic to the monolithic application. It might seem trivial to do at first, but things can go really bad in live environments, especially in mission critical services, like pizza metadata. Make sure to practice the playbook as well, and involve other teams to review it.

- Logging and monitoring should be in place - Your logging and metrics should be in place and properly monitored during the release time, both on the monolith, the new service and the databases as well.

- Choose the time and place - Ideally, such a release should happen during a low traffic time, you know your application best, so choose the time accordingly. Monday mornings or Saturday mornings are usually a good choice for such migrations in general. If you have the chance, have people from the owner team and (if exists) the platform team on premise for efficient communication.

- Practice on staging - Something that many teams forget is that there's usually a pre-production or staging environment for their system. You can utilize this space to practice the release a couple of times, since there's ideally no real customer data there.

- Let the rest of the company know - This is a crucial step, make sure that public relations and the customer care team know about the maintenance that is coming up and the possible impact on customers. The more they know, the more effectively they can communicate if something goes bad.

- Don't forget about the data - Make sure that you have a plan for the data backfill as well, since it's possible that during a problematic release, there would be data discrepancies between the monolith and the microservice database.

Here's an example playbook for reverting the **tizza** application under fire. The goal is that the people who are doing the release don't need to think about anything, just follow the instructions.

1. Prerequisites:

   a. Make sure that you're connected to the **VPN**.

   b. Make sure that you have access to **http://ci.tizza.io**.

   c. Make sure you have ssh access to the requested machines.

   d. Have the latest **https://github.com/tizza/ tizza** cloned on your machine.

2. Announce on **#alerts** channel with **@here** that there's an issue with your release and a revert is required.

3. Visit **http://ci.tizza.io/tizza/deploy**

4. Select the version of the application that you'd like to deploy and hit the green button.

5. If the deployment tool reports failure, continue.

6. **ssh** into the host machines, you can use **ssh -A <host ip>**

7. Run the following commands:

   a. **sudo su -**

   b. **bash -x ./maintenance/set-application-version.sh <application version>**

   c. **supervisorctl restart tizza-app tizza-nginx**

8. If the service still doesn't respond, call +36123456789

This playbook is quite simple, however, it offers multiple options for the developer to fix the situation. It includes a prerequisites part, so the developer who runs these commands can make sure that they can do everything that the playbook requires. It also includes a catastrophe situation solution, where a phone number is provided, which is most likely linked to an experienced developer in the field.

There's also a communication plan for the rest of the company as the second step. This is absolutely crucial, since the rest of your company will be interested if something went amiss.

We've done it! The application is migrated, however, we are not quite ready yet. The most fun part is still coming up. Let's talk about how to make sure that we don't leave a huge mess behind.

Cleanup

The graphs and logs look great. Customers are not complaining about any new issues, the system is stable. Congratulations, you've just released a new microservice! Now comes the most fun: cleaning up the mess that we've left behind.

Just like you would do with your kitchen, make sure that you don't leave behind unwanted things in the old codebase. You can take your time with this, as a matter of fact, it is usually a good idea to leave the old code in place for 2-3 weeks, so if there are some issues you can still revert to the old logic using the playbooks that you've created.

After your new service matured for some time, make sure to go through the following cleanup checklist:

- Turn off replication between the monolith and the microservice databases - If you haven't already, you can turn off the data replication between the two databases now.

- Remove unused tables from the new service - If you went with a simple full database replication, you can now delete the tables from the microservice's database that are not involved in the domain. This should free up plenty of storage.

– Remove unused code from the monolith - Time to
remove the modules that are not used. Make sure to
do a clean sweep,utilize tools like **pycodestyle** to find
unused code that can be removed.

– Remove unused tables from the monolith - Now that
you're certain that no code accesses the tables that
have been migrated to the new service, you can safely
drop them. It might also be a good idea to archive this
data and store it for a while, doesn't cost much.

Conclusion

We've learned a lot in this chapter about small techniques that you can use
to speed up your microservice migration. We've also made a huge mess
in our new system in the meantime. There's a lot of duplicated code and
it's still not clear who is owning what parts of the application. In the next
chapter, we are going to dig deeper in this conversation and make sure that
we can not just increase the number of services we have, but also scale
our organization and the development for optimal efficiency with these
systems.

CHAPTER 6

Scaling Development

So far we have spent a lot of time with the how and why of designing and building microservices. However, there is this age old principle that many industry professionals have coined throughout the years, which says that "code is read more than written." This is true for infrastructure and systems as well. If you want to make sure that your systems scale so people understand them at a glance and can move on quickly to the "writing" part of software engineering, you need to spend some time working on tooling and culture in your organization. In this chapter, we will explore some of these areas.

Using Python Packages

One thing that I mentioned a couple of times already is that we've been working with a lot of code duplication during the hypothetical migration that we did in the previous chapter. Every software engineer knows about the DRY principle (if you don't, look it up right now), so hopefully some of you felt uncomfortable duplicating this immense amount of code.

In this first part, we are going to look at an alternative way of reusing code. By using Python packages.

© Akos Hochrein 2019
A. Hochrein, *Designing Microservices with Django*,
https://doi.org/10.1007/978-1-4842-5358-8_6

What to Reuse

The first question you might ask yourself is what you should create a new package for? The answer is the usual: whatever code exists in two or more microservices should be migrated into a separate package. Sometimes there are exceptions for this, for example, if you expect heavy code drift in the duplicated code on the short or long run, you should keep them in separate services and let them drift apart. Some of the examples that we've worked on in this book that should go to separate packages:

- RabbitMQ publisher and consumer - The base code for these should be the same in every service, thus they should have their own package.

- Bearer token authentication method for the rest framework - In chapter 4, we've also looked at the option of bearer token authentication for the Django REST Framework. This should also be distributed in a package, since if it changes in one place, it should change everywhere.

- Rate limiting middleware - In chapter 3 we've had an exercise to create a middleware that would limit the calls based on the IP address and the amount of calls over a time period.

- Remote models and their instances - The models described in chapter 5 are an excellent item to distribute in a package as well. If a model has changed in the system, the owner team just needs to update the client accordingly and re-distribute the package.

There are, of course, other examples as well. If you have a custom date module for your systems, you might want to distribute that as a package as well. If you have Django base templates that you'd like to distribute around the services, packages are perfect for you.

Creating a New Package

After you've decided which module you would like to move into a package first, you can start the migration process by simply creating a new repository in your favourite code management tool. Before this, however, it is highly recommended to check what internal and external dependencies the module has that you'd like to move out. Packages depending on packages whilst not handling backward-compatibility usually cause trouble on the long run and should be avoided (especially if the dependence is circular, in that case, avoid it at all costs).

If you've isolated the code you'd like to move out, you can create a new repository and migrate the code that you'd like to have in a separate package. Make sure to move the tests as well, just like you did when you migrated your services. After the migration, you should have the directory structure shown in Figure 6-1.

auth-client-python
- tizza
   - auth
      - ...
- tests
   - ...
- setup.py

Figure 6-1. *Basic package directory structure*

Let's go over it file by file:

tizza - The directory we would like to keep our package source code in. You might wonder what happens when there are multiple packages? The answer is that the Python module system handles same name modules pretty well and loads them as you would expect. It is generally a good idea to have a prefix like your company name as a prefix for your packages, since it can be a very good indicator in your imports, whether a particular method came from a package or not, also, it can be a good way of marketing your company if you'd open-source these packages in the future.

tests - The directory where we will keep our test source code in.

setup.py - The package file that holds meta information about the package itself. It also describes how to work with the package and what are the requirements of it. These files are very powerful and can do many operations around you package. I definitely recommend checking out the documentation at `https://docs.python.org/3.7/distutils/setupscript.html`. Listing 6-1 is an example **setup.py** file:

Listing 6-1. An example setup.py file for a package

```python
from setuptools import setup, find_packages

VERSION = "0.0.1"

setup(
    name="auth-client-python",
    version=VERSION,
    description="Package containing authentication and
    authorization tools",
    author_email='akos@tizza.com',
    install_requires=[
        'djangorestframework==3.9.3',
    ],
    packages=find_packages()
)
```

As you can see, it's quite simple. The name attribute contains the name of the package itself. The version is the current version of the package, it's moved out as a variable so it's easier to bump it. There's a short description and there are the dependencies required by the package. In this case, version 3.9.3 of the Django REST Framework.

Using a new package is no more difficult than creating one. Since pip can download packages from various code hosting sites, like Github, we can simply insert the following line into our requirements.txt file:

```
git+git://github.com/tizza/auth-client-python.git#egg=auth-client-python
```

Running **pip install -r requirements.txt** will now install the package as it was intended.

One more thing we can mention here is about package versioning. Earlier in the book we've mentioned that pinned dependencies (the ones with fixed versions) are usually better than unpinned ones, due to the control that developers receive over their systems. Now, here, as you can see, we are always pulling the latest version of the codebase, which goes against this principle. Luckily pip supports specific package versions, even if they are coming from a code versioning system and not a "real" package repository. The following pins are allowed: tag, branch, commit and various references, like pull requests.

```
pip install git+git://github.com/tizza/auth-client-python.git@master#egg=auth-client-python
```

Luckily, releasing a new tag is quite easy, you can do it with the bash script in Listing 6-2:

Listing 6-2. example bash script for publishing tags

```
#!/bin/sh

VERSION=`grep VERSION setup.py | head -1 | sed 's/.*"\
(.*\)".*/\1/'`
git tag $VERSION
git push origin $VERSION
```

This script fetches the version information from your **setup.py** file and creates a new tag from it in the repository that you're in, assuming that the structure is the same as of the file above. Thus, after running the script, you can use the following in your requirements files:

```
git+git://github.com/tizza/auth-client-python.
git@0.0.1#egg=auth-client-python
```

Which is quite convenient when we would like to work with pinned packages.

Note   Tagging is a great tool for managing package versions, however, in an ideal world, you would not like your developers to be taking care of this manually. If you have the resources, you should add the tagging logic into the build system's pipeline that you're using.

We have set up our package, time to make sure that it's well-maintained with tests.

Testing Packages

In an ideal world, testing your packages should be simple and elegant, running a single test command, which is most likely the one that you've been using in your monolithic application, where your code resided originally, however, sometimes life is just a little bit more difficult. What happens if your package needs to be used in environments where the dependencies are different from each other? What happens if multiple Python versions need to be supported? Luckily, we have a simple answer in the Python community for these questions: **tox**.

tox is a simple test orchestration tool which aims to generalize how testing is done in Python. The concept revolves around a configuration file called tox.ini. Listing 6-3 shows us a simple example of it:

Listing 6-3. Simple tox file

```
[tox]
envlist = py27,py36,py37

[testenv]
deps = pytest
commands =
    pytest
```

What this file says is that we would like to run our tests against Python versions 2.7, 3.6 and 3.7, with the command **pytest**. The command can be replaced with whatever testing tool you are using, even with custom scripts that you've written.

You can run tox by just saying: **tox** in your terminal.

What does this mean exactly? Well, when you're developing software at a company which operates with multiple Python versions across the ecosystem, you can make sure that the packages that you're working on will work in all versions.

Even from this short section you can see that tox is a great tool for maintaining your package. If you'd like to learn more about tox, I recommend checking out its website at `https://tox.readthedocs.io/`.

Now that we have an understanding about packages, how they should be structured and tested, let's take a look at how we can store meta information about our services, so developers at the company have an easier time finding the information they need in the fastest way possible.

Service Repositories

As your system grows with more and more microservices, you will face different issues that you've faced with your monolithic application. One of these challenges is going to be data discoverability, meaning that people will have difficulty finding where certain data can be found in your system. Good naming conventions can help with this on the short run, for example, naming the service that stores pizza information **food-service** or **culinary-service** might be a better choice than naming it **gordon** or **fridge** (however, I do agree that the latter two are more fun). In the long run, you might want to create a meta-service of some sort, that will host information about the services that you have in your ecosystem.

Designing a Service Repository

Service repositories always need to be tailored to the given company, however, there are a couple of things that you can involve in the model design by default to get started as shown by Listing 6-4.

Listing 6-4. Basic service repository models

```
from django.db import models

class Team(models.Model):
    name = models.CharField(max_length=128)
    email = models.EmailField()
    slack_channel = models.CharField(max_length=128)

class Owner(models.Model):
    name = models.CharField(max_length=128)
    team = models.ForeignKey(Team)
    email = models.EmailField()

class Service(models.Model):
    name = models.CharField(max_length=128)
    owners = models.ManyToManyField(Team)
    repository = models.URLField()
    healthcheck_url = models.URLField()
```

We kept it quite simple here. The goal that we are aiming for is enablement for teams and engineers to communicate with each other. We created a model that describes an engineer or owner in the system and we've created a model that describes a team. In general, it is better to think of teams as owners, it encourages these units to share knowledge inside the team. The teams have a slack channel attached to them as well, ideally it should be a single click connection for any engineer to get information about a service.

You can see that for the Service model we've added a couple of basic fields. We've set the owners as a many to many field, since it's possible that multiple teams use the same service. This is common in smaller companies and with monolithic applications. We've also added a simple repository url field, so the service code is accessible immediately. In addition, we've added a health check url, so when someone is interested if this service is working properly, they can do it with a simple click.

Having the basic meta-information about our services is great and all, but now it's time to add more every-day-use content to it.

Looking for Data

Now, as we've started this section, one of the most interesting metadata that an engineer can look for is the location of a particular entity that exists in the system and how to access it. For our service repository to scale in this dimension, we will need to extend the codebase of the already existing services as well.

Documenting Communication

The first thing that you can ask your teams to do is to start documenting their communication methods. What this means is that for every service for each team, there should be some form of documentation that describes what entities, endpoints and messages exist for the given service. As a starter, you can ask your teams to have this in the readme of their service, but here we are going to take a look at more options.

The Swagger Toolchain

For API documentation, there are a lot of tools on the internet to look at, the one we will be diving deeper into is called Swagger. You can find more information about Swagger at `http://swagger.io`.

The Swagger API project was started by Tony Tam in 2011 in order to generate documentation and client SDKs for various projects. The tool has since evolved into one of the biggers RESTful API tools that is being used by the industry today.

The core of the Swagger ecosystem is a yaml file that describes the API that you'd like to be working with. Let's take a look at an example file in Listing 6-5:

Listing 6-5. Swagger file example for the pizza entity

```
swagger: "2.0"
info:
  description: "Service to host culinary information for the
  tizza ecosystem: pizza metadata"
  version: "0.0.1"
  title: "culinary-service"
  contact:
    email: "team-culinary@tizza.com"
host: "tizza.com"
basePath: "/api/v1"
tags:
- name: "pizza"
  description: "Pizza metadata"
```

```
schemes:
- "https"
paths:
  /pizza:
    post:
      tags:
      - "pizza"
      summary: "Create a new pizza"
      operationId: "createPizza"
      consumes:
      - "application/json"
      produces:
      - "application/json"
      parameters:
      - in: "body"
        name: "body"
        description: "Pizza object to be created"
        required: true
        schema:
          $ref: "#/definitions/Pizza"
      responses:
        405:
          description: "Invalid input"
  /pizza/{id}:
    get:
      tags:
      - "pizza"
      produces:
      - "application/json"
      parameters:
      - in: "path"
```

```
          name: "id"
          required: true
          type: "integer"
      responses:
        404:
          description: "Pizza not found"
definitions:
  Pizza:
    type: "object"
    required:
    - "name"
    - "photoUrls"
    properties:
      id:
        type: "integer"
        format: "int64"
      title:
        type: "string"
        example: "Salami Pikante"
      description:
        type: "string"
        example: "Very spicy pizza with meat"
```

So, the file contains some meta information about the service and the owners of the service in the beginning. After that we define the endpoints that the clients can be working with, we even mention the base urls and the paths that should be used.

Each path then is broken down to methods, you can see that we have a POST method assigned to the pizza/ endpoint for pizza creation. We also describe the possible responses and what they mean, including the structure of the pizza object at the end of the file. The definitions also include what type of data is accepted and can be returned from certain endpoints. In this case, all our endpoints only return application/json as a response.

At first glance, this file just looks like some unreadable nonsense. However, when you pair it up with the rest of the Swagger ecosystem, you will receive something marvelous. As a starter, the file in Figure 6-2 that was created by a visual editor can be found at https://editor.swagger.io.

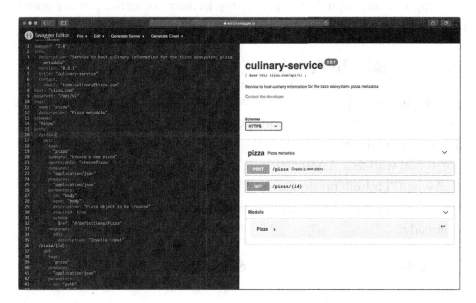

Figure 6-2. The swagger editor

The Swagger editor is a dynamic tool with which it is very easy and fun to create Swagger files. It also validates the files to the Swagger format, this way you can make sure that your API descriptor files stay inside the ecosystem.

You can also leverage the Swagger UI (the right panel in the image above) in your own systems, you can download the source code and host it next to the service repository if you please, giving you ultimate power over your API descriptors and the people who want to learn about this.

The first thing that you might ask yourself is if there are any ways to generate client side code from these definitions. The answer is yes. Swagger has a code generator module that covers the generation of client side code to multiple programming languages, however, we will not be

151

discussing these options in this book. If you'd like to learn more of these tools, I recommend reading the code and user manual at https://github. com/swagger-api/swagger-codegen.

Swagger is absolutely fantastic for synchronous APIs, however, it does not support many asynchronous features. In the next section, we are going to learn about another tool that can help us with that.

The AsyncAPI Toolchain

Similarly to your synchronous APIs, you can (and should) document your asynchronous APIs as well. Unfortunately, Swagger does not support definitions for protocols like AMQP, however, we do have another excellent tool to deal with this, **AsyncAPI.**

AsyncAPI is built on similar yaml files as Swagger is. Listing 6-6 displays a simple example for the culinary service that we've been working on already:

Listing 6-6. AsyncAPI example descriptor file

```
asyncapi: '2.0.0-rc1'
id: 'urn:com:tizza:culinary-service:server'
info:
  title: culinary-service
  version: '0.0.1'
  description: |
    AMQP messages published and consumed by the culinary
    service

defaultContentType: application/json

channels:
  user.deleted.1.0.0:
    subscribe:
      message:
```

```
  summary: 'User deleted'
  description: 'A notification that a certain user has
  been removed from the system'
  payload:
    type: 'object'
    properties:
      user_id:
        type: "string"

pizza.deleted.1.0.0:
  publish:
    message:
      summary: 'Pizza deleted'
      description: 'A notification that a certain pizza has
      been removed from the system'
      payload:
        type: 'object'
        properties:
          pizza_id:
            type: "string"
```

The specification here is quite simple. We have two routing keys, one for user deleted, which we consume and one for pizza deleted, which we produce. The structure of the messages is described in the message themselves, however, we can also create objects similar to the ones in the Swagger description file.

Just like in the synchronous world, we have a nice editor UI (Figure 6-3) that we can work with here as well, found at https://playground. asyncapi.io.

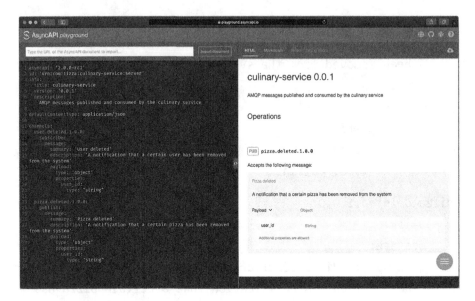

Figure 6-3. The AsyncAPI editor

Note   As you might have seen, we did not declare which exchange the messages would be published to or consumed from. The **AsyncAPI** specifications have no native way of describing this, however, you can always add an **x- attribute** for this case. Now, we can call it **x-exchange**. Which the specification accepts.

Time to place our new shiny API descriptors into our service repository.

Tying it Together

After these files are in place, we can start linking them into our service repository. Listing 6-7 shows you how to add them as extra fields to the Service model.

Listing 6-7. Updated service model

```
class Service(models.Model):
    ...
    swagger_file_location = models.URLField()
    asyncapi_file_location = models.URLField()
```

These new links will enable us to have instant access to user interfaces of APIs in all of the services that we have. If we want to, we can also extend the models to contain and periodically load the contents of the urls, which we can index to be searchable on the user interface.

Other Useful Tields

Now, if you have this amount of data available in your service repository, you are already doing quite well regarding industry standards and are providing very advanced tooling for your engineers to navigate in your complex microservice architecture. There are a couple of fields that you might want to add in the future, so I will leave some ideas for you here that you can improve in the future:

Graphs, alerts and tracing - An easy addition to your service repository could be to add your graphs, alerts and the tracing information for your service. These are usually simple URLs, however, if you want to go super fancy, you can always embed the graphs into some UI elements, so the developers who are exploring services have an understanding of the service's status at a glance.

Logs - Maintaining and working with logs is different for each company. However, sometimes it can be difficult to discover logs for a given service. You might want to include documentation, a link or even the log stream itself (if possible) of your service into the repository itself. It might speed things up for engineers who are trying to figure out if there's an issue with the service, but are not very familiar with it.

Dependency health - Since the great scandal of the JavaScript ecosystem of 2016, when half the internet broke because a dependency (left-pad) got disabled in the node package manager, there is a huge emphasis on dependencies, and you might want to get on the train as well. There are tools that you can use to determine how up-to-date and secure your dependencies are in your service. You can use **safety** for this, for example.

Build health - Sometimes it can be useful information if the build pipeline of the service is healthy or not. This can also be displayed on the service repository UI if needed.

As you can see, service repositories can be very powerful tools not just for service discoverability, but also to give a good overview about your ecosystem's health and overall performance.

In the final section, we are going to take a quick look at how we can speed up developing new services with the power of scaffolding.

Scaffolding

We've gotten quite far in how we can scale our applications development-wise. There is one small step that we still might want to do before concluding this book, and that is scaffolding services.

One of the ultimate goals that you can be aiming for when designing a microservice architecture is enabling teams to deliver business logic as quickly as possible, without interruptions on the technical domain. Meaning that setting up a new service (if required by the business) should be a matter of minutes and not a matter of days.

The idea of scaffolding services is not very new. There are many tools that can enable you to write as little code as possible and click as few times as possible on the interface of your cloud to spin up a new service that your developers can work with. Let's start with the former one, as that is quite close to what we've been working on.

Scaffolding the Codebase

When we are talking about scaffolding code, we are talking about having a directory structure with various placeholders in them and replacing the placeholders with template variables that are relevant to the service. Designing a base template for your service is not at all difficult. The main goal that you want to achieve is to keep is as minimalistic as possible, while maintaining the tech specific requirements that should exist in every service. Let's see a list of what these can be:

–   *Requirements files* - Most services like maintaining their own requirements, so it is generally a good idea to maintain these in every service separately. There are some teams which like maintaining their requirements in base images for their services, that can also be a solution for this.

–   *Tests* - Teams should write tests in the same way, meaning that the folder structure and execution for unit-, integration- and acceptance tests should be the same everywhere. This is required so developers can get up to speed with a service as soon as possible. No compromises here.

–   *Base structure of the service* - APIs and templates of a service should look the same in every service. The folder structure should feel familiar to everyone in the company who works with the given language, there should be no surprises when navigating the codebase. This structure should also work in itself and should contain something that works just after the templating is finished.

- *Base dependencies* - Probably implied by the requirements files, however, I would like to put an emphasis on the base dependencies. The main goal with these dependencies is to keep common code intact and not have it be rewritten by multiple teams in the company. The packages that you've extracted before should come in the base dependencies and if they are not needed, they can be removed in the long run.

- *Readmes and basic documentation* - The base template should also include the place for readmes and other documentation files, such as Swagger and AsyncAPI by default. If possible, the script that will work with the template updating should also encourage filling out this information in some way.

- *Healthcheck and potentially graphs* - The scaffolding of the service should also include how the service can be accessed and how it can be checked if it's working. If you're using tools like Grafana that build service graphs using JSON descriptor files, you can generate them here as well so the base graphs look and feel the same for all services.

- *Dockerfiles and Docker compose files* - We have not talked much about Docker and the ecosystem around it in this book, however, if you're working with these tools, you should definitely make sure that the services you're scaffolding include these files by default.

The base scaffolding should be accessible to everyone. I recommend to create a new repository in your favourite code versioning system with the template and the script that will fill up the template in it and have it accessible for all developers in the company. You can also leave up an example service for clarity if you'd like to.

For the scaffolding itself. I recommend using very simple tools, like the Python **cookiecutter** module.

One thing that I'd like to note here, is that scaffolding will speed you up in the short run, however, it can cause another set of problems in the long run. Making sure that all these files that we've generated stay uniform and interchangeable across the entire microservice ecosystem is near impossible. At this point, if you'd like to work with a healthy and maintainable infrastructure, it is a recommendation to put dedicated people to work on the unification and operational scalability on your systems. This recently booming culture in engineering is called "developer experience." I recommend researching it and evaluating if adaptation is worth it for you and your company or not.

Scaffolding the Infrastructure

Scaffolding the codebase is one thing, another thing is making sure that there are resources in your cloud provider to be able to host your systems. In my experience, this area is extremely different for each company in each cycle of the company's lifetime. So, I will provide some guidelines and mention some tools that you can use here for your convenience.

Terraform by HashiCorp -Terraform is an incredibly powerful tool for maintaining infrastructure as code. The basic idea is that Terraform has various providers defined, such as Amazon Web Services, DigitalOcean or the Google Cloud Platform and in these providers all resources are described in a JSON-like syntax. See an example terraform file in Listing 6-8:

Listing 6-8. A simple terraform file

```
provider "aws" {
  profile    = "default"
  region     = "us-east-1"
}
resource "aws_instance" "example" {
  ami             = "ami-2757f631"
  instance_type = "t2.micro"
}
```

The above example comes straight from the Terraform website. It shows a couple of lines of code with which you can create a simple instance on Amazon. Pretty neat, huh? For more information on terraform and tools to scaffold your entire infrastructure, you can head to http:// terraform.io and start checking out the tutorials.

Vault by HashiCorp - After a while, you will notice that not just the management of your code and services can become a difficulty, but also the management of your secrets, passwords, usernames, keypairs, in general, everything that you don't want to share with people outside your business. Vault is a tool created by HashiCorp to make things easier in this area as well. It provides a simple interface and integrates well with the rest of the cloud ecosystem. The API around it is simple and secure.

Chef - One of the most popular infrastructure as code solutions, Chef is used by hundreds of companies across the globe, such as Facebook, to power up their infrastructure. Chef uses the power of the Ruby programming language to scale.

Conclusion

In this chapter, we've taken a look at how we can work with Python packages and how we can use them to make sure that the wheel doesn't get re-invented by our developers every single time they are creating a new service. We've also learned about service repositories and how we can help ourselves by creating detailed documentation of our synchronous and asynchronous messaging systems. We've also taken a look at scaffolding services and what are the minimal requirements for the templates that we would like our engineers to use when they are creating new services.

I hope that this chapter has provided useful information to you on how to scale the development of microservices in your organization.

Index

A, B, C

Asynchronous communication, 94
  broker outages,
     handling, 106–109
  GDPR solution, 94
  message payloads, 104, 105
  outbox architecture, 107
  queue, concept, 95–97
  RabbitMQ, 97, 99
    consumers, 101–103
    producer, 98–101
    routing keys, 100

D, E, F, G, H

Data preparation
  database duplication, 122, 123
  domain sharding, 117–121
  migration, 119
  Python properties, 121
  testing, 122, 123
Dependency inversion
    principle, 59–60
Django project, 13
  admin panel, 30–33
  AuthenticationMiddleware, 38
  CommonMiddleware, 38

directory structure, 16
folder structure, 15
installation, 14
liking functionality, 39
login and logout, 33–37
middlewares, 37, 38
ORMs (*see* Object Relational
    Mappings (OMRs))
permissions, 43–45
random pizza, exercise, 27
REST
  authentication, 88–94
  caches, 92
  cookies, 92
  database, 92
  routers, 82–87
  serializers, 81, 82
  settings.py file, 80
  view sets, 82
SecurityMiddleware, 38
signing up, 30–33
templates, 39
  code explanation, 41
  pizza shuffling endpoint, 42
  source code, 39, 40
Tizza, 13
views of communication, 24–27

© Akos Hochrein 2019
A. Hochrein, *Designing Microservices with Django*,
https://doi.org/10.1007/978-1-4842-5358-8

T, U, V, W, X, Y, Z

Printed in the United States
By Bookmasters